UNIVERSAL TRUTHS MANUAL

Awaken to Who You Truly Are and Create Your Heaven on Earth

AMANDA ABELSETH

**FAMILY OF LIGHT
TEACHINGS**

ISBN: 978-0-9937718-4-2
FIRST EDITION, MAY 2015

Editorial supervision: Kelly Lamb

The material used to create this book was supplied by an FSC certified provider and the interior is comprised of 30% post-consumer waste recycled material. All material has been obtained through responsible sources.

This book is dedicated to my husband and soul mate. Without his love, support and encouragement, I would be lost.

This book is also dedicated to you. Without you, this book would not have been called into existence.

TABLE OF CONTENTS

CHAPTER 3 – CREATING YOUR HEAVEN ON EARTH

PREFACE
By: Amanda Abelseth

As I sit here to write my part of this amazing channelled manual, I wonder what I can offer you that could be of assistance. To try to write something as an introduction to these life changing teachings is, well, not an easy thing to do. But as I sit here, I recall one of the primary messages of these teachings: **our example is the most powerful tool**. Through my example, I can inspire you to want changes in your own life and encourage you to awaken the inner knowing that will get you there. So what I will give to you is a brief testimonial of my experience with these teachings and my sincerest hope that you gain as much from them as I did.

Before beginning my work with our Family of Light, I had no idea where my life was heading. Although I have always had my ability to channel, I blocked out my guidance in my early years and assimilated to "normal" existence. Throughout my life I unknowingly called upon these natural gifts to receive guidance for myself and others, but with no understanding of the channelling process, I just assumed it was always a strange coincidence. It wasn't until 2012 that I – like so many others – began to awaken to the truth of my existence. And not long after, I unleashed the full scope of my natural channelling abilities. Our Family of Light began to speak to me frequently, and their presence was undeniable. After battling with the idea that I might have to commit myself, I finally went online and did my research. It wasn't before long that I discovered what was really happening to me and realized what a blessing this experience was. Surrounded by the loving support of my Guides, Angels and the Ascended Masters, I acknowledged my channelling ability and began the journey of releasing the blocks that were programmed into my mind long ago.

Shortly into my awakening, the Ascended Masters informed me that I was ready to start the next phase of our work together. I was told that I was going to channel a series of books called "The Light Manuals." For some this may have seemed liked a daunting task, but I was overjoyed and could not have imagined a better purpose. Well, that's what I thought at first. I tell you, our Family of Light really had their work cut out with me. I struggled immensely with my Joy to complete this work and my overwhelming fears that I couldn't do it, I wasn't good enough and that maybe I WAS actually making it all up. But as I began to channel the first book and study what they had written, I realized I was merely a textbook case of their teachings. A fearful woman plagued by my limiting beliefs, as a result of my programming. I recognized how many others must feel like me – insecure, uncertain and wanting answers – and I was compelled to move forward. I began to follow the teachings diligently, and as I sit here now, I am in awe of my progress.

So what have I achieved through these teachings?

I began this reprogramming journey fearful, as a woman with a temper due to childhood abuse issues. I did not know how to love, but more accurately, how to allow myself to be loved. I was scared of trusting anyone and eager to blame others for my misfortune. I often sabotaged good things in my life due to my low Self-Worth and found myself obsessively clinging to those that loved me, expecting them to bring me happiness. I couldn't truly let anyone in, and I had no idea what I was going to do next. My fears and anxiety had become so overwhelming that I was not enjoying my life. I was simply watching it pass by. I always managed to get the resources I needed, although it was frequently through copious amounts of hard work and struggle. I was able to manifest a reasonable life, but it was one that reflected my inability to allow abundance and peace on the mental plane. I had what I needed – just enough to get by. My physical reality was a perfect reflection of my mental state of struggle, lack and fear. It wasn't until I began following these teachings that I accepted the idea of change and started to let go of my fears. I realized that life did not have to be the way I was living it and that there was something important we were all missing – precious knowledge that the majority of us had all forgotten. Truth was awakening within me, and I was on the precipice of great change.

After incorporating these teachings into my life, I am proud to say that the woman I once was has transformed and expanded into a completely different version of Self. Although I am not perfect and still struggle with my own limiting beliefs at times, my personal Self Expansion is truly amazing. I am confident and secure in myself and my path. I no longer feel the need to blame others for what happens in my life and have accepted my power over my reality. I have learned to trust and have faith in the knowing that I am capable of achieving anything. My relationships with others are no longer based on insecurities and the need for affection, and instead, they are blossoming into pure companionships, full of trust and acceptance. My life with my family has expanded into more love and Joy than I could have ever imagined. As I have allowed myself to accept love from others, I have found a rekindled, passionate and unique relationship with my husband, as well as a deep connection and adoration for my children. I have truly discovered peace within my own existence and found a profound sense of gratitude for every step along this journey. And if that were not enough to make these teachings truly priceless, I am also quickly learning to master my physical reality and all the resources within it.

One of the dominant themes of this manual is that you are capable of receiving any resource you desire. What we require to achieve our desired path is not only in reach, but can be attained without copious amounts of physical work and mental exercises. What this manual teaches is that creation is a part of you and not something that you need to work for mentally or physically. It teaches you how to relax, create effortlessly and spend more time enjoying your creations, instead of trying to force them into reality. Using these teachings, I have completely transformed my life. By incorporating this powerful knowledge into my everyday life, the resources I desire for my personal life, as well as my global purpose, flow effortlessly into my experience. I am manifesting the resources to live my life on my terms and am happy to say that I am breaking free from archaic manmade rules and systems.

As I have allowed true Joy and peace upon the mental plane, I have witnessed beautiful miracles and abundance flow into my physical reality. The fact that the physical is a mirror to the mental plane has become undeniable in my life, and with these great truths, I have begun living my Heaven on Earth. My sincerest hope for you is that you find the same peace, freedom and Joy within your own life. I trust that you will take what you need from these teachings and that when you are ready, you will emerge as the Joyous Conscious Creator you are meant to be. As I have given my example to you, it is your purpose to fulfill this same function and show others the truth of their potential. Through our example, we will show the world a new way of existence. We will shine the light of truth and awaken others to the knowing within them.

Enjoy the channelled teachings that follow. As these lessons have been recorded in a 30 day reprogramming format, you will achieve optimal results by reading one lesson per day - allowing your Self time to review and reflect before proceeding. May you find peace and Joy within them and awaken to who you truly are!

All of my love and support,

Amanda

INTENTION

This manual has been written with the greatest intent of light,
the greatest intent of healing and the greatest intent to bring
peace, Joy and ultimately Heaven on Earth.

These lessons serve the great purpose of bringing forth that
which the Collective Consciousness is now ready to receive.

Behold, we offer you a key to unlock the greatest Truths you will ever know...

THE PREREQUISITES

WHO WE ARE

We would greatly enjoy the opportunity to formally introduce ourselves before we commence with these most important lessons. Who we are is not something that is easily understood by the physical mind, but we will do our very best to explain our existence in the simplest manner. Who we are – is you! In reality that is the truth, but the physical mind perceives only individuality, and so we come to you representing a collective of beings known as the Brotherhood of Light.

The Brotherhood of Light is not gender specific and exists as a collection of Ascended Masters, whose sole intention is to serve the physical world in its Ascension. We are not human, so to speak, but as aspects of our True Selves, we have been in physical form at one time or another. We are those that have ascended in previous lives and much like your Self, we have chosen to remain tied to the physical world until she has Ascended, as was intended. We do not represent individual identities in this manual; instead, we represent every deity, every great master and every teacher that you have ever admired. If it pleases you to refer to us as a great spiritual leader you respect, this is most Joyous; as we represent the many faces of your greatest physical teachers.

We are a collection of beings who are proud members of the Family of Light, and we come to you today through these beautiful words to deliver a most important message. We come to bring you the truths that we promised we would bring you. We are fulfilling our part in the nonphysical, as you are fulfilling yours in the physical. We bring you this message because you have called for our assistance and because it is only together, as a united Brotherhood of Light, that we will succeed in our great mission. We offer you these words as not only our perspectives but as the perspectives of your Higher Self. As we are one in our intentions, our perspectives and ultimate truths are very much the same.

We encourage you to read these words and allow their resonance to fill every ounce of your being. We know that in hearing this message, you will feel at home and undoubtedly reconnect your precious energy with ours. You are us and we are you. We are one, dearest being, and we welcome you home now, as an elite member of the Brotherhood of Light.

THE GREAT ILLUSION

We will begin this manual with an understanding of the illusion you find your Self in. Only in having this illusion brought to your attention, will you begin to see the holes within it and allow your Self to broaden your mind and receive the truths. We will begin where one must always start – at the beginning of it all. Your science and authority figures have taught you many wonderful details about your Selves and your existence. You have been taught about the mechanics of the universe and the way the human body works; in addition, you have even been presented with proof of all of these amazing discoveries. Your science has touched on the truths, in so many ways, and yet has only begun to grasp the reality of All That Is. This is what you know about existence, according to what society has told you:

You are born as a little fish, one of billions, swimming in the large ocean that is your planet. You are brought into a world where you are taught to believe that you are but a slave to the circumstances and conditions you are born into. If you are so lucky, you will find your Self born into a family of wealth and privilege and be afforded luxuries that will allow you to make something of your Self. If you are not as fortunate, you will be born into a "lower class" family, where you will undoubtedly be faced with struggle, years of debt and few opportunities to make anything of your Self. The conditions that determine which family you are born into is out of your hands, and you are simply born where you are born. Society, as a whole, frowns on the idea of thinking that you have any real say in what happens to you. You are to believe that it is merely luck or chance that determines your good fortune. You are simply to follow the rules, pay your taxes, get your nine to five job and assimilate to the "happy" existence that is the human dream.

Your science talks about the human race as if it were some sort of fluke, much like your own individual existence. A sort of happenstance that allowed your species to find itself where it is. A "big bang" that resulted in life, that resulted in evolution of said life and so forth and so forth, until you found your Self as these modern physical beings that you see today. Your science says that there are rules in The Universe, but that in actuality all that exists was really created out of chance.

There is little hope among your society, about practically everything in your physical world. The animals are dying; the planet is dying; this will give you cancer and that will give you cancer. If you don't happen to be struck by one of the millions of cars your technology has created to "simplify" your life, you are most likely to be the victim of a violent assault, as a result of your increasing crime rate. Or perhaps, you will be hit with a bout of depression like so many others, consequently due to the shared overwhelming sense of loneliness and insignificance. Not to worry, however, you have your sciences that can fix your wounds and prescribe you plenty of little pills to solve whatever ails you. You perform your daily functions – much so like a robot – following the rules and doing what you are told. Until one day it is all over. You either succumb to illness, old age or some sort of tragic event, and then, boom, that is it, no more you.

At the moment of your death, many believe you briefly reflect on your life. You look back at all the choices you made and all the choices you should have made. You look back on loves that you let walk away, on those you hurt and on the things you wish you could have said; you look back with regret, longing to do things differently. You look back wishing you could have seen how very precious this life was instead of "sweating" the small stuff. You wish you had more of the moments of Joy, more of the moments filled with laughter and true love. Moments that made your heart sing and moments that brought you closer to a sense of fulfillment. Well, friends, we are here to tell you – and to show you – that all things that could lead to regret are avoidable now. All that you will eventually come to wish you had enjoyed, all that you will wish you had experienced is yours for the taking NOW. We are here to tell you that this mundane robotic existence of a life based on chance and unfair circumstances IS the Great Illusion. You are NOT meant to be born out of chance and pulled through life via the circumstances that happen into your experiences until you meet your eventual death. The greatest illusion of all is that you are only human: a fragile life form that is destined for birth and then an inevitable death, where you will forever cease to exist. This is the greatest injustice of all. For believing this denies the Truths of who you truly are and what you are capable of. Let us now explain the Truths.

THE UNIVERSAL TRUTHS

You are an infinite being. You are born into your life of your own free will, and when you choose to depart said life, you continue to exist as something far greater than the physical form you see before you. You are not your body or your mind; you are a pure energy source and you are one with All That Is. You are a Divine Creator, a child of the Infinite Source, and you are capable of anything. You are not a tiny fish wandering aimlessly in an ocean; you are a mighty being who has chosen to incarnate on this planet so that you may experience physicality. As you are, as the physical being before you, you are but a form that houses a much greater energy. You are the avatar for the True You that exists outside of any perceived space and time limitations, an infinite being that has existed and will exist for all time. You have come into this space-time continuum so that you may grow and expand and forever change the course of All That Is.

The world you see before you is not as it appears. There is form, that is undeniable, but even form is not as it appears, as will be explained in these lessons. There are no rules, except the rules that you place on your Self. The inaccuracies that you have been told about your physical capabilities and the stories you have been told about your insignificance, have been grossly exaggerated. You are not a slave to circumstances; you are not defined by the situations you are presented with. You are a master of these circumstances. You are meant to determine all of your experiences, and you are meant to create whatever reality you choose. You have simply forgotten your ability to do so.

Your science has taught you undeniable truths about the physical world you see around you, but there is so much more to reveal. You exist on a plane of form – a solid plane of slower vibrations, which offers a tangible product to touch and taste. To experience your world, your physical body provides wonderful sensory tools, which allow you to collect information. You are designed to be a life form that is capable of extensively experiencing all aspects of physical reality through your senses, but again, there is so much you have forgotten. You see, your reality does not merely consist of a physical plane of tangible form, and your sensory tools are not merely comprised of the five senses that you are most commonly made aware of.

The physical reality you see around you exists as one of three planes and is known as The Physical Plane. However, there also exists the Mental and Spiritual Planes, upon which all of the behind the scenes work takes place to create that which is seen on the physical plane. You are continuously working on the mental plane and are always in contact with the True You on the spiritual plane. Your body is equipped with far greater tools for data collection than just your five basic senses. Every cell in your body is created with built-in sensors that are able to detect, analyze and interpret infinite amounts of energetic impressions from people, places and things all around you. Now understand that we only use this separation, of "people, places and things," simply because this is the way your mind perceives the world; however, in reality, you are no different than these places or things that you perceive. You are one with nature, with the waters and the plants, and you are one with all beasts that walk upon your planet. Again, you have simply forgotten.

You are far greater than you give your Self credit for, and your body has been designed with capabilities far beyond that which you currently acknowledge. We will teach you how to use all aspects of what is available to you. We will teach you how to consciously operate within all Three Planes. We will teach you to use the senses correctly – including your ability to interpret all energetic impressions – and we will show you how the information collected thus far has deceived you. We will teach you and in doing so, remind you of that which you already know. You will come to remember that there is so much more to your existence than you currently realize and while you re-awaken to this knowing, we will eagerly remain by your side watching as your journey unfolds. We promise you, as you read these words, experiences will unfold, perceived coincidences will flow into your reality and you will undoubtedly see proof of the Universal Truths. Enjoy this process and **Awaken to Who You Truly Are!**

WHO YOU ARE

YOU are the current version of Self. As you grow, expand and collect data, this version of YOU is continuously upgraded, producing an ever evolving Self. The Self is comprised of three components: Body, Mind and Soul. The body is the form you see before you, the mind is the operating system of the Self program and the Soul is the programmer – Higher Self and the True You. YOU are not your body or your mind; YOU are Higher Self experiencing through the body and the mind, as the physical aspect known as: "Insert your name here." You are Self.

~It is by the light that the Truths are revealed and fears of the darkness dispelled. For the darkness exists as merely hidden Truths and in the light the Truth is made clear.~

CHAPTER 1
THE AWAKENING

CHAPTER 1
INTRODUCTION

As you read this, you may find that your life is not precisely where you imagined it would be. You may feel as though you have failed; that you have not succeeded in meeting the societal requirements that are deemed necessary to be considered successful. Well friends, brothers and sisters, we are here to tell you that everything you have been told and everything you have perceived with your physical eyes and ears is an illusion. In fact, every bit of information you have gathered about the world you live in has been inaccurately interpreted by your physical senses. You have been trapped in the fantasies of your programming for too long dearest ones, and it is time now to awaken! It is time to strip away all illusions that have blinded you from the truths, and it is time to remember.

We will begin this journey by reminding you of who you truly are and awakening you to your purpose in this life. We will begin by slowly lifting the veil and allowing you to peak beneath the curtain. Doing so, in a slow and progressive manor, will allow your eyes time to adjust to the Truths. We will begin gently, but we assure you when you are ready, you will move eagerly beyond the veil that has shrouded your eyes, and you will walk fearlessly into the new world. We will begin this journey together, and we will remain beside you at all times, offering guidance and wisdom. We will commence this journey hand in hand because it is together – united – that we will succeed. To our brothers and sisters, it is time to awaken. It is time to remember who you are: that which cannot be destroyed and that which lives on eternally from this life to the next. You will remain beyond your physical body as energy, and you will continue to remain for all of eternity.

This is where the first lesson will begin: with an understanding of infinite Energy and the all-encompassing energetic forces of the Universe. We will awaken you to understandings that your science and your schools do not teach. For if they did, if they truly understood all that we will teach you, there would be no teaching institutions like you are used to. For the students of today, having been given the key to the Truths, would quickly outgrow their teachers, and they would surpass them in understandings and knowledge, long before the allotted education time period. For the individuals that exist today and the souls that reside within them, within you, are far more ambitious than your predecessors. You see, your predecessors were not meant to achieve what you will achieve in this lifetime, as it was simply not their intention to do so. Only in this time period have generations intended to come forth with such knowing, with such force and brute strength, to tear the lid off of all mundane and archaic institutional ideas. Ushering in a new light of understanding and forever changing the world. And so, your schools, institutions and limiting teaching aids cannot assist you in finding that which you truly seek – because within their walls, the truth does not lie. The Truth lies within you waiting to be unlocked; waiting to be beckoned forward and ONLY YOU can bring this knowledge forward for you. We will hold your hand through this process, allowing new data to flow to you that will reprogram the mind and essentially debug the erroneous thought patterns that you have gained from your authority figures. We will walk with you and ensure that you receive the necessary key to open the door for your Self and discover the Universal Truths.

This will not be an effortless journey. We will not lie to you and say that it will be pure sunshine and rainbows, but what we will say to you is that it will be the most rewarding journey you will ever take. So sit back; hold on tight and awaken to the truth. Sit back, but do not relax your guard; be ever vigilant. Set your intentions correctly and direct your thoughts accordingly. This may be a bumpy ride at times, but it will be worth every moment. We are with you now and always. Enjoy the journey!

LESSON 1
ENERGY

To begin our journey together, we will open with a discussion of fundamental knowledge that must first be appreciated to grasp the concept of all that we will teach you. We will begin by examining the core of all life and the Source of All That Is: Energy. What is energy exactly? What does this word mean? To most people using the English language, it merely represents concepts like electricity or, from a broader perspective, any source of power. However, energy to our understanding means something far greater, and today we will begin by broadening your interpretation of this profound word.

When you look around you, what do you see? You see solid objects; you see finite objects that have a definite shape. You see physical objects that would remain in the same state unless some force, be it your Self or a machine, imposed a change upon them. Well, what we will explain to you now will help you understand that there is far more to that object, to that supposedly solid structure, than meets the eye. As we have said before, you cannot trust anything that has been collected with the physical senses, and so this will be your first lesson.

Let us choose an object now. Let us observe this object. What do you see? You see a solid structure, but within that structure lies the basis of ALL form and ALL life in the universe. This solid object that you see before you is in fact not solid at all; it is an ever moving, ever transforming, ever vibrating object that only appears solid when perceived with your physical senses. In reality, this object is a mass of revolving and vibrating particles that have, in their dense and lowered vibratory state, come together to create said object. When you break down the solid object using scientific instruments, one can clearly see that this object is not, in realty, solid at all. So what does this mean? What does this suggest?

We will go further with this and examine for a moment the physical body? If the physical body is of the physical world, then this must suggest that the physical body is subject to the same composition as all other physical objects. In truth, the physical body is comprised of the exact same make up of all objects in the physical world on a subatomic level. What does this suggest then? If say a table and a human body are no different, what does this suggest about the world itself? Does this suggest that all physical manifestations, be it man, animal and object alike, are merely molded objects out of a universal clay or universal energy? Would this not then infer that man, although he perceives himself as superior, is in fact no different than the table he eats off of and the road he walks on? Could this imply that the physical body that you see before you is only a product of the physical world, used to operate within the physical plane? And expanding upon this, is it possible that "You" are something much more than the physical form you perceive as the reflection of you?

These can be complex and profound questions to ponder, but let us now move forward and discover what makes you different from inanimate objects, such as a table or a road. Yes, you are made of the same elements as these objects, but you would certainly not say that you are the same as them. There is something within you that is different, something that separates you from all objects. It is your consciousness, it is the "You" essence. The part of you that allows for thoughts, for emotions and for consciousness. So from this understanding, we must then address why it is that if you are comprised of the same elements as a road, do you have a consciousness and the road does not? This is the primary question to be answered. IF you are structurally made of precisely the same elements as all other physical world objects, then what is it that resides within you that separates you from them, and, more importantly, why are you separated? This question is of course one that cannot be satisfied with a simple answer, as it is a complex answer indeed, and to address this question, we must return to the core of this lesson; we must continue to examine energy.

Now as we have stated, from the average person's limited understandings of energy, they would perceive that it is merely the transfer of particles; simply what powers the world and makes trinkets operate. But what is energy really? Well, it is what makes up the entire world. It is the universal power source that creates ALL and resides within ALL form and ALL life. It is the tables and the roads, it is the trees and the plants, and it is you. Energy is all these things, and yet it is so much more. Energy is that which cannot be destroyed. It is infinite and unalterable in its most basic form. So when we address who YOU truly are, the answer is quite simple: the True

You, the consciousness beyond your physical body, is Energy, of course! You are infinite, and you cannot be destroyed or altered in your most basic form. So you ask, "Okay, if I am energy as the True Me and my body is energy, what is the difference between these energies? If all is energy, then why do I sense a separation between my body made of energy and my consciousness made of energy?" Well, this is what we would like to discuss now. What separates your energy body from the life force energy that flows within you, if essentially all energy is the same? Well, this answer may surprise you, or perhaps it may not. The energy that creates your physical body and the physical objects you see around you IS no different than the life force energy that resides within you; they are one. It is this oneness that you must first come to understand. You are a separate life force, a consciousness made up of sacred energy, but in the same sense so is a road, a table, the plants and the animals. You are all one – made from the same infinite and indestructible energy.

Let us move forward with these understandings. If the Self and the consciousness are the same energy as the table before you, then what is the point? Why is there separation? Understanding the need for separation is key, but to truly understand this "separation," one must only perceive it through the eyes of oneness. You must first acknowledge the infinite energy that abounds in the Universe and resonate with the knowing that all is one and the same. When you embrace this, you will then be ready to understand not the differences or the division between your Self and the rest of the physical world, but you will begin to comprehend the union between your Self and the world. You will begin to see that everything around you is YOU and resides within you. You will begin to appreciate nature and understand that everything in nature is to be respected, as you would respect your Self. So with this understanding, we can now address why there is a perceived separation, from a "non-separate" perspective. We can now address how you are more than the energy that creates the physical tangible world. Now understand, we mean "more" not in the sense that a table is "below" you, because in reality it is not, but we mean this in the sense that you are a more complex expression of the same energy that resides within said table.

So then, what is different about you that makes your energetic expression more complex than all other expressions in the universe? Well, it is the intention of your existence. A table is simply a table, a chair, a chair. They were created to be nothing more than the objects that they were intended to be. They were never intended to walk about, to examine the world and to jump around and sing. They were intended to be tables. You on the other hand were created with a greater purpose. Your body was created as a means of expression for your Soul, your higher nonphysical Self and the True You, so that you could have experiences in a physical world. The energy that created your Soul was directed via the intention to produce an infinite, indestructible and conscious growth seeking being that would evolve through experiences in this world and the next. Your physical existence is dependent upon your growth, and when your growth and expansion is complete, you will begin yet another phase of growth and expansion, as was the intention for your creation. And so, what is the difference between you and a table, between your physical body and the soul that resides within you? Nothing but intention.

Now, in order to take this discussion where it must go next, it is essential that we discuss a topic that may be considered taboo to some: this topic of God. It does not concern us if you believe in "God" or not. The fact of the matter is that you must believe in an aspect of the Source for this process to work, for it is essential to becoming a Conscious Creator. Will this "God" be depicted as a man on a throne floating around on a cloud, will he be depicted as an ever watching judge who condemns those that do not bend to his will, or will the concept of God encompass something far greater than the limits set forth by organized religion? The choice is ultimately yours, but we would love to give you our understanding of God. We would love to give you new insights and allow you to comprehend how we perceive the Source Creator. We ask for a moment that you release any preconceived notions that you may have as a result of your upbringing, and we ask you to purely listen. To us, our God and our Creator cannot "simply" be conveyed in words. The Creator is the alpha and the omega, the cause and the effect. God is both the beginning and the end and as these are but one and the same, God can simply be explained as What Is and as existence itself. The Creator cannot be summed up in mere words and cannot truly be understood with the physical mind. The Creator is neither male nor female and does not exist as an omnipotent man who will punish you for your sins. These images are your creations for God; they are not God.

God IS energy. God is a life force – the battery, if you will, that fuels all things, physical and nonphysical, that exist in the Universes. God is and resides within all that you see around you and all that exists beyond your world. God is the building blocks that creates form and the energy that breathes life into all things. God IS All That IS. And yet even in saying these things, we have failed to express the true magnitude of the mighty Source Creator. As we have said, it is very difficult to sum up all that the Creator represents in a mere paragraph. It is not necessary to debate about what the Creator is or isn't. It is simply essential that you recognize that there is an ultimate Source to All That Is. When this is fully accepted and embraced, you will understand your true power. And so we ask that when you think of your Source Creator that you remove all limiting beliefs. Remove any limiting ideas or notions that you received from any and all religious sects, as these are not representative of God. As we have said, these are manmade depictions of the Creator. These limiting concepts are the projected fears of those that so greatly dreaded their own condemnation that they created a punishment for their perceived sins: one that could not be escaped. We want for you to understand, as we have repeated, anything and everything collected with your physical senses is an illusion.

Now that we have addressed what must be addressed and discussed what was inevitable to discuss, let us put this all together. We have explained that you are a part of the infinite energy that creates all life and all form, and we have conveyed that all energy comes from the Source Creator. Now we must address why? Why is this all happening? Why are you here? Why has this bountiful energy come together in such a way to create the world you see around you? The answer is far simpler than most imagine. It has come together because we, the collective, have deemed it to be so, as we desired the opportunity of growth for our boundless souls. We have asked our Source Creator for the opportunity to experience the physical worlds, to prove our ability to become conscious Joyous creators. The world exists as it does because we have willed it to be so. These understandings may seem brash for a first lesson, but we assure you these are essential understandings for what is to come.

These understandings are the foundation for you to realize your power and your ultimate potential in this world. Do not fear this concept of a Creator and this concept of your place in All That Is – embrace it. Through embracing your power, you will begin to understand your true place in this world, and you will begin to allow the infinite creative power that resides within you to be unleashed. We will begin the next lesson by discussing precisely who you are and why you are here.

LESSON 2
THE GREAT QUESTION

In this lesson, we will discuss a topic that has plagued man for millennia. We will address the question that drives copious amounts of tests, research and scientific study around the world: the great question – why? "Why are we here? Why does this all exist?" These are questions that in themselves invite the asking of a vast array of subsequent complex questions such as: "What are we here to do? Who are we really?" These questions have become the catalyst for the endeavors of many. We will attempt to address questions such as these from a new vantage point and, in doing so, offer you new perspectives. We will do so to show you the Truths that exist before your very eyes. Perhaps you have heard somewhat similar theories from your scientific community, but we assure you, your science has only grasped a small fraction of the truths that we will teach you.

Firstly, it is essential to understand that you do not fully grasp the true reality that exists around you. Your eyes do not see the millions upon millions of photons that race past you at every moment. Your eyes send this data back to your brain, but as result of filtering, the brain only processes a small fraction of what the eyes are actually seeing. There is so much more to your reality than you realize. So much more that exists in front of your eyes that your brain simply ignores. We would like to begin to allow you to see more with your physical eyes and allow you to receive more input from your physical brain. So we will begin where we must first begin, so that an adequate level of understanding can be achieved. Let us begin with an understanding of why all that you see before you exists. As addressed in the previous lesson, we have communicated that you and all that you see before you exists simply because we collectively have deemed it to be so. All of us that help on the other side, as your ascended brothers and sisters, and all the souls that reside on the planet have all decided that Earth was to be. We recognize that this response will not solely satisfy your need for answers, and so we will elaborate. Why does Earth exist and why are you on it, you ask? Well, to be more specific, you are on Earth as an experiment, as a great test and learning opportunity for you, Higher Self. The Earth exists as a school, if you will, with the potential for boundless growth and expansion!

In reality, you are an infinite being – an endless presence comprised of pure energy. You do not have a physical body. And so a plan was devised, an arrangement was plotted, so that you could expand your experiences and expand your being to allow for a physical existence. This was done for you, as it was done for all of us. This occurred eons ago and was not a decision taken lightly. When the decision was made that we collectively desired to exist on a physical plane, the very moment it was conceived, it was done. Time does not exist linear as you perceive it in your world, and so the moment we intended for the creation to be – it was. And so now you ask:

"Okay, so we decided to come here. What are we here to do? And what exactly did we want to learn?" Well, we simply wanted to collect experiences. After all, that is what our entire existence consists of: the continuous collection of experiences. From your perspective, these experiences are viewed as past, present and future experiences; however, from our perspective, we do not use time in this linear manner, and so we simply say that we have experiences in general. These experiences are essential for our personal growth and as growth seeking beings, we would want nothing less for ourselves. The decision to become physical was merely an opportunity to learn and expand our intentions, to allow our souls experiences that were not possible from a purely vibrational nonphysical state. This was a most Joyous experience for us, and despite how the world may appear in the present moment, this was our choice and one that we embraced eagerly.

When you wonder why this world is the way it is, and when you wonder why it appears that humans have fallen so far as a species – please remember that this was our choice. It was our decision to take on this test, and we are all doing precisely what we are meant to be doing. Although this may be hard to hear and may drum up numerous thoughts such as "Why do some suffer and some do not," it is not yet time to discuss these things. For now, let us leave these thoughts and address them at another time. We do understand that there might be numerous questions bubbling to the surface – many questions that you feel need to be addressed and that you believe are essential for your understandings. We assure you, friend, with patience and diligence, you will discover the necessary solutions within these lessons. Remain faithful to these words and study them with vigor and dedication, and you will find the answers that you seek.

Now we must address the next burning question: "If we came here to learn and if we came here to embrace growth, when are we done?" This is a most important question. One that cannot be understood with immature knowledge. This is a question that will be answered over the course of many lessons, but we will begin by stating: you must remember, first and foremost, that your energy is never ending, and as growth seeking beings, your learning will never cease – not even beyond this physical life. So we ask you to remember that this is but one phase of learning for you, and when your time is done here – when you have passed the test of this physical life – you will embark upon a new test. Please do not look at this life as crossing your last finish line. This is one of many finish lines for you. Relax and enjoy the ride, and do not be so eager for a completion – as a concentration primarily on the completion, and not on the steps required, will result in perceived failure.

To continue with this most important lesson, we will commence with your understandings of who you are. At this point, you comprehend the prerequisites. At this point, you understand the very basics and have only begun to scratch the surface. These limited understandings will soon be expanded beyond your wildest imaginings, and we ask that you embrace what we will convey with open minds and open hearts. When you ask the question of who you are, there is not a simple answer. There is not an answer that will appease your mind, because at this moment you may not be ready to truly embrace that which you are. Even though we will tell you now, it will take much convincing throughout these lessons for you to truly grasp that which you are. At first, you will not fully comprehend the true extent of the power you hold and the true extent of your abilities, but in time, you will come to accept the Truths of who you truly are.

To further delve into an understanding of who you are, we will briefly recap what you have learned. So far in these lessons, we have explained to you that you do not understand all things in your world. You have realized that energy is not as you perceived or at least what you were taught in school and that energy is much greater and all encompassing. Until this point, you may not have understood the intentions of energy and the complexity with which it formed itself into shapes and solid structures. You may have only vaguely understood the world around you, but of course this is as it was meant to be. You may have known your entire life that there was something else out there, that this world seemed off kilter and out of balance. You may have realized that there was much more to the bland reality you have been fed by your authority figures. You knew, but you just couldn't put your finger on it. As of now, all that we have told you is that you exist in this world by your own choice; that you exist with the intention of growth and expansion. We have explained that you exist with the purpose of gaining experiences, and through these experiences, you intend to ascend from this plane of existence into another plane, where you will continue on another path or set of intentions for growth and expansion; all part of a never ending process.

We are pleased with your understandings of these concepts, but what we will address now is much more pressing. It is the understanding of who you are. Who you really are. You are a creation of Source Energy; a child of God, if you will – created as a royal family to live in absolute peace and Joy. And so from this perspective, we will move forward. As these children of God, as these direct descendants of Source Energy, you your Self have been bestowed with amazing gifts and abilities. You have a power within you that is of the True Source, which allows you to create your own reality and the reality of the world.

The latter is the very essence of these lessons; the very essence of what we will teach you. But to understand this, to understand how to create the life you desire free of that which you do not want, you must first accept the obvious. If you your Self are an extension of the True Source, if you are a child of God, then you your Self are like God. You stem from the same energy of the Divine Creator, and you are a Creator. As was the intention for your conception. This concept can be difficult for many to hear: that they have power within them that can create worlds, power that stems from the ultimate Creator, but we assure you this is the Truth. Take note of any limiting beliefs regarding this notion, any insecurities and thoughts of impossibility that YOU could hold such power. Be not afraid of them, as it is these thoughts that we will reprogram. It is these concepts that must be addressed and rewritten so that you may become a Conscious Creator. With these limiting beliefs, you hinder your own abilities and you deny your birth right. However, with them rewritten and with the full embracing of who you are, you will create a world so marvelous around you that others will be in shock and awe.

We are so pleased to be on this journey with you. It fills us with absolute Joy to see that you are seeking, that you are asking to discover who you are. Even though these words may seem foreign to you, like you are reading a fictional novel at times, deep down you will know that this is the Truth. For Self is prodding you to walk forward; encouraging you to embrace your power and walk onward without fear.

LESSON 3
YOUR ROLE

In today's lesson, we will begin by briefly recapping what we have come to understand together. From your current perspectives, all that we have learned may not be fully absorbed. We mean this in the sense that it may not be time for you to fully allow your Self to embrace what we have taught you. And so in this process, you may find that we must repeat the same concept to allow for adequate understanding. Please know that every word we speak, every single word, is reprogramming your mind. Every word, every repeated thought, serves the purpose of adding programing that will allow your mind to eventually run a new version of Self. So we ask you to bear in mind that all words are essential, all thoughts are necessary, and it is all part of the master plan.

Okay, what have we learned? You understand what energy is. You understand where energy comes from and the basics of why you are here. It may appear to be heavy topics to begin with, but the fundamentals must be understood and will be covered more extensively in later lessons, when you are ready. And so where do we go from here?

We believe it is essential to now move onto your specific purpose in this world. Yes, you are here to gain experiences and to gain perspectives for your continual growth and expansion, but of course, there is much more to your purpose. There are those that incarnate on the physical plane, whose sole intention is to release themselves of their created karmic ties via multiple different lives and various experiences. They are finding their peace, their Joy, and they are re-emerging their essence with the Source. When their time is done, they graduate from "Physical World School" and they ascend, achieving all that was desired from the experience of a physical existence. And then there are others; others like you. Those that have chosen to stay behind. Those that could have ascended after previous lives, but have selflessly donated their time to ensure that the rest of the family ascends in a timely manner. You are one of these people. You are here to assist in the Ascension process of the planet. You have been called many names: Lightworker, Light Bearer, Architect of Light, etc. But it matters not what you are called, for you are simply an Advocate of Truth. You are a bearer of the Light of Truth who has chosen to come forward to dispel the illusions of the "darkness," or more accurately "the unseen Truths." The fact of the matter is that you are not only here to raise your vibration or consciousness to a point of Ascension after this life, you are also here to assist others and to serve the great purpose of illuminating the world. Through your work, mighty Lightworker, you will see to it that the world moves gracefully through this great period of mass Ascension.

Now to best understand what you are here to do, it is most important to truly understand who and what you are. These are understandings that are difficult to explain in a mere paragraph, but we will begin this journey of Self Expansion by telling you what you need to know to open the door – revealing the Truth of your existence. You are the equivalent to an Ascended Master. Though your names may not have been known throughout human histories, you are a great Ascended Being, who has incarnated on Earth to assist in her Ascension. The fact is that all of you who will find this manual and learn from its teachings, have gone through some form of Ascension on this physical planet or another. You are experts, if you will, and you have chosen to come forth because of this expertise. Some of you are practicing the extraordinary capabilities that you were born with and some of you are not, as many of you chose to immerse your Self so deeply into the world of illusion for the role that you intended to play. Neither role is superior to the other, for both roles are serving their function, and each being holds great power beyond physical world comprehension, whether currently dormant or not. There are so many of you now that are awaking to your true nature, and in time, you will come to understand all that you are and where you have come from. But for now, know this: you are an expert. One well versed in overcoming the illusions of physical life, and you are here to assist others in doing the same through the process of their awakening.

You may have felt this calling already. You may feel drawn to assist others. You may feel that there is something within you that draws you to run to the aid of others or offer your services whenever necessary. This is your true nature, as you are here to assist. You may find along this path that although the strong desire to make a difference in the world prods at you, programming from your parents, schools and authority figures has left you with a "bad taste" in your mouth, so to speak. You may find that although you desire to help the world, there are times when you are merely sickened by the practices that have become so common place, and you wish some days that you could shut your Self away. On the opposite end, there may be some of you that already view the world with compassionate eyes and simply take on any challenge knowing that you can and will make a difference through your presence.

It matters not which person you are, because the fact is whatever category you fall into does not define you as a "good" or "bad" Lightworker. What category you fall into defines the type of work you are here to do. Please know this: if you find that you are having a hard time in the world, this is most wonderful! We do not mean this in the sense that we enjoy your suffering. We mean this in the sense that this indicates that you will have ample conflicting data that you will inevitably overcome, and in doing so, you will be a well-rounded teacher. You will be experienced and versed in the illusions of the world, and you will be a teacher of true knowledge that will be able to relate and show the world, through your own example, how to overcome all "perceived" problems.

For those of you that currently embrace the world as it is, your nature and your charisma is so very much needed. Through your good natured attitude and your strong light, you have been changing the world with every thought and every word, and you will serve a most important purpose as a healer. Your focus on seeing the positive in all situations allows you to easily transmute the negative energies of all that exists around you. Your work is equally as essential, and although your role appears different from that of the teachers, the difference is only superficial.

When we separate Lightworkers into two categories, Teacher and Healer, this is simply for explanation and clarification purposes. In reality, all functions performed by Lightworkers are a form of healing. Whether it be healing the mind through the reprogramming of data or healing the body in some form, all healing work is essentially the same. Likewise, all healing is a form of teaching, designed to show the Truths of our existence and awaken knowing within. All is targeted at bringing perceived "darkness" to the light and transmuting it, regardless of the form it has taken. Whether you are an energy healer, an advisor, an author, a physical healer, a builder of the new world or whatever form of healer/teacher you choose, it matters not the "title" you give this work. Just know that your purpose goes far beyond a personal goal for growth and expansion. You are not here with the primary intention to graduate and ascend like so many others. You are here to change the world and provide an environment for a mass graduation, unlike anything the world has ever seen. You are a "called in" expert, one who is well versed in overcoming the illusions of the physical world. You are a master, and you have already overcome your own version of ascension. You are here to eliminate old patterns and old institutions. You are here to bring forth a new way of living and a new way of viewing the world. Through your example, you will heal the world and awaken those around you with your actions and validations.

So now let us take a break; let us take a step back. For those that find these words strange. For those that think these words seem so science fiction and based in an alternate world that is not part of your reality, we ask you to consider for a moment: what is it that you even understand about your reality? What do you know? What do you think you know? What exists in your understandings, in your collected data, that was truly learned by you? We would like for you to address the fact that all things that you are aware of and all data that has formed your perspectives, exists in your mind as others have intended it to. Your authority figures, your parents, your teachers and your governments have downloaded copious amounts of data into your mind that has resulted in your current thought patterns. And so we ask you: what is it that you really know? What you know is what they have taught you, what belonged in their thoughts. They taught you their perspectives, their beliefs and their limited knowledge. It is time for you to learn your own perspectives, perspectives of your choosing. It is time for you to embrace what you truly know.

If these words are difficult for you to process, we encourage you to walk away for now. Walk away and think on it, but we assure you the time WILL COME when you return. Because deep down you know that this is accurate information; you know this is the Truth. You know this because deep down it resonates with every ounce of your being, and it is only your limiting beliefs holding you back. Know that you are not asked to disbelieve everything you have been taught by society; we are simply asking you to re-examine EVERYTHING. We are asking you to re-evaluate what you have been taught and to review every bit of data you have collected with your physical senses, because it is these physical senses that have misled you. It is perceiving the world with limiting eyes that has gotten the world precisely where it is. So when you begin to question if this is merely a trick, merely a too good to be true fantasy, please remember that the world that you think you know – the world that you have been "taught" to believe in – only exists the way it does for you because you have been conditioned to believe in it. You did not willingly learn these rules, these stipulations for life. They were programmed into you.

We ask you to give these lessons your full attention. We invite you to give them your full acceptance, and the door will open for you revealing knowing beyond your wildest imagination. You are not asked to be perfect, but you are asked to be vigilant. You are asked to watch your thoughts and trust the thoughts that feel right to you. Trust the thoughts that trigger knowing and intrigue within you, and DO NOT trust the thoughts that conjure up fear, doubt or worry. These thoughts, known as fear based thoughts, are of the Ego Self, and this is precisely where our next lesson will begin: with a discussion on Higher Self and the Ego Self that you have created.

LESSON 4
THE EGO SELF

Today it is imperative that we begin one of many lessons on the subject of what we choose to refer to as: the Ego Self. There have been many names given to this "ego" and there have been many understandings placed on it as well, but we wish to offer a rarely considered perspective. To begin, we wish to address that which must first be recognized, for one to truly embrace True Authentic Self and rid themselves of the Ego Self completely. What must first be addressed is that in reality there is NO EGO. In your culture, your psychology has proceeded to create numerous fragmented versions of your psyche. You have your Id, your Ego and your Superego; your illusory Self fractured into numerous parts so that you can explain why you act the way you do without having to take accountability. While we do appreciate compartmentalizing to determine how and why a situation is occurring, we do not feel that it is beneficial to dwell on these understandings for long periods of time. Doing so only furthers the idea of a compartmentalized and fragmented mind, and so we will ask that you look at your mind in a different manner.

When we ask you now, what is the ego? What is the understanding of "ego" to the average person? You might respond that it is merely the part of you that is self-interested, the part that sticks up for you and is driven to bend you to its will to make you selfish and self-centered. The concept of egotistical, if you will. Well, in a way, this understanding is correct; but in a way, it is only scratching the surface of the truth. This ego belief that you have, the idea that you have a part of you that is making you act selfishly against others, this is the part that we will address first. First and foremost, we want you to remember that in reality there are no parts to your mind, let alone any unwanted parts that you cannot control. There is simply SELF. You are SELF. The exact "makeup" of Self will be discussed in greater detail during another lesson, but we will simply state you are your Body, Mind and Higher Self. All three components make up your AUTHENTIC SELF. This will be explained in further detail when your mind is ready to understand and fully appreciate the concept.

For now, let us simply discuss the mind. When we refer to the mind, it is best understood that we are talking about the "mind" in the sense of this trinity that makes up your Authentic Self. To discuss this mind, we must begin by allowing you to understand what occurred many eons ago that resulted in this fractured mindset. There was a time when you existed as purely vibrational; this was a glorious time of peace and tranquillity. Then came the descent, in which you vibrationally descended to allow your Self to exist physically.

During this physical existence, it was imperative that to ensure your survival, you be fitted with a defense mechanism that would allow your body to tell you when you were hungry, when you were tired, when you felt that the physical body was threatened, etc. This was your built-in "defense mechanism." This defense mechanism resulted in what has now become known as the "EGO."

We will explain in further detail. This defense mechanism was neither good nor bad, it was simply a means by which the physical body was protected and cared for. The physical body was able to easily communicate what it needed so that the mind was able to provide. And this worked flawlessly, but over time, a degradation occurred. The mechanism went "out of whack" so to speak. This idea of the body needing to protect itself morphed into needing to defend against fellow brothers' and sisters' bodies, thus, creating a need to fight for survival and for supplies – as a result of the introduction of the fear based intentions of separation and scarcity. This was extremely challenging for you; this was challenging for all. This concept of scarcity did not exist in your pure vibrational state, where there is no need to eat or no need for shelter; but in the physical world, the fear of these needs encompassed your thoughts. And so this great separation occurred. This separation where you began to feel a need to compete against your fellow incarnated souls. This began as small incidences, and eventually a fear so great rose up within you that the trinity of Authentic Self was no longer working in correct order; the mind had become disconnected. As was our intention for the created mind to operate with Higher Self as its "director," the mind was unable to exist without a conductor telling it what to do. From this lack of direction sprang the creation of the Ego Self. As an aspect of its creator, the mind was able to instantly create a new conductor the moment it required direction. Because this Ego Self was created as a result of a disconnect from the unconditional love, safety and knowing of Higher Self – the mind's new conductor was cruel, unaware and completely fear based.

And so we say that this Ego Self – this creation – was not merely produced as a means to shelter the body, it was created as a means to attack against all others. It is not a defense mechanism; it is the very epitome of separation and fear. The Ego Self arose from fear and a need to defend Self against all others, and so it is no wonder that any thoughts of distress, jealousy or loathing stems not from Higher Self but from the Ego Self. This created concept encourages you to pit your Self against your brothers and sisters, due to the fear of a supposed threat to your existence or a perceived lack of supplies. At the very moment you choose separation, you forget your power, you forget that you are a Conscious Creator, and you forget that you have the ability to create anything you desire.

To further understand this concept of the Ego Self, it is important to fully embrace that the Ego Self is NOT REAL. It is your mind's creation and is constructed from the data in your mind. The collected data from your senses, stored in your mind, shows you that life can be hard on this planet and that you need to compete for food, compete for money and compete for love; you are always needing to compete. This is what you have been shown at least. In reality, however, you are a Creator and so anything that is created by you cannot be taken by another – it is your creation. And so we say that the original separation that was initially perceived long, long ago, is no different than what occurs every day when new babies are born and raised to believe the fears that fester around them. Still to this day, people choose fear. They choose to allow Authentic Self to be disengaged, they choose to allow the mind to create a new driver, an Ego Self, whose primary goal is to take the wheel and drive you into its own version of hell. It is derived and created out of fear and hatred, so it can only operate under the assumption of fear and hatred. Please remember that this is not you. This is a created illusion of your making that you can so very easily do away with at the time of your choosing. This is what we will discuss in the next lesson: how to understand and recognize Ego Self vs. Authentic Self operation, as well as a basic understanding of how we are going to eliminate the Ego Self once and for all.

LESSON 5
THE EGO SELF – PART II

In reference to the Ego Self, it is first important to understand that this creation – produced by you – has been greatly misunderstood by the masses. Even those that come to understand that the Ego Self is a creation of the mind, fail to understand that even the acknowledgment of an Ego Self is an injustice to the Self. The very acknowledgment of its existence, continues its existence. Many who are awakened and sense the presence of this false Self spend years battling with this perceived enemy, trying desperately to control and tame a beast of their making. We will not do this; we will go straight to the heart of the matter. We will work on purging this limiting creation from the get go so you can learn efficiently and focus on controlling your thoughts – as opposed to controlling a fictitious devil.

Today we will discuss the differences between the Ego Self and the Authentic Self in greater detail. This Authentic Self that you are, this immaculate functioning system, works flawlessly on its own as Body, Mind and Soul. It is a great system that filters through only thoughts of love, Joy, pure happiness and bliss. And so you ask, "When do I know that I am operating as Authentic Self?" Well, we say in every moment of true Joy and true bliss. In the moments that your eyes well with tears of utter happiness; in the moments where you truly feel that you are so completely whole. It is in these moments where your connection as Authentic Self is at its strongest. Now this is not to say that you do not connect to Authentic Self on other occasions, but you may find that these connections are often tainted by limiting data, causing energetic blocks or fears. This is something that we will discuss in great detail in lessons to come. For now, let us work on simply finding the Joy. Do not be concerned if you find that negative thoughts creep up while you experience this Joy. We will work on that hand in hand in due time. For now, simply focus your attention on being happy and on doing whatever it is that makes you happy. As beauty is in the eye of the beholder, so is Joy. Remember this and do not let ANYONE tell you what your Joy should be. This Joy that you seek, seek it with all that you are, and first and foremost, remember to always keep Joy within your thoughts. For you are about to learn that it is your thoughts that hold the power to create Joy in all aspects of your life. It is through the mind that all things come to be in the physical. Nothing can be brought into your reality without it first being thought of in the mind. Allow us to examine this notion further.

The Ego Self is a construct of your mind, comprised of and fueled by the limiting data collected via your physical world senses. Yes, this is most true; but we wish to take this another step further. This Ego Self is so very different in the nature of the Authentic Self in another very important way: the Ego Self wishes you the experience of "death." This may seem so very bizarre of a concept, but it is in fact the Truth. To properly understand these concepts and to rightfully be a Conscious

Creator, you must first see the Ego Self for what it truly is and what it truly isn't. In doing so, you will begin to see what is happening within your mind and truly embrace with perfect knowing that you have the power to control every thought.

What do we mean when we say that the Ego Self wishes you the experience of "death"? We mean precisely what we say. It is through this belief and fear of a pending death that the Ego Self wins. For you see, through this process of illness, Self-destruction, death and the continual disassociation with the True You, Ego Self keeps you tied to the illusion of your fictitious tyrant leader and ensures its continual existence. Through the illusion of "death," the Ego Self continues to exist beyond the physical; reborn in the next life as part of the souls rebirthing process. The Ego Self will continue with each successive life, until eradication of the Ego Self is achieved and Ascension occurs. Or more simply put, when the illusions of the physical world are overcome and the student is ready to graduate. Remember, you created this Ego Self out of a sense of separation and as a dueling counterpart to Higher Self. And so this dual opposite, always in opposition to Higher Self, must of course play the part that you intended for it. Such is the purpose of the illusion of duality – good vs. bad, and opposites always in opposition. You called forth a master of separation and division from your brothers and sisters, and what better way to keep you from seeing your true oneness and connection to All That Is, then by keeping you in time with the illusion of death and never allowing you to see your true nature. For in reality, there is no death – there is only life – continual and infinite life! When you see past the illusion of death and see the Truth of infinite life, you supersede the Ego Self and reach a true state of oneness and enlightenment.

The Ego Self is your creation; yet, it has become your master, because you have allowed it to be so. Let us address a scenario and paint you a picture of what occurs consciously for many and unconsciously for others. The Ego Self has its own survival at heart and as the fictitious devil, it tricks you and encourages you to do things that will ultimately lead you to harm. At times, you may feel you are alone with no one else to turn to and so you entertain the ideas of this devil. Time after time, you learn to accept this devil, and you learn to believe that no one else is assisting you, and at least this devil has kept you safe and secure for this long. After all, this devil has allowed you to see everyone else's true nature. You know that they are deceitful and cruel, that they think bad things of you, and that they would take from you, if you were not to take first. This devil has protected you by reminding you of the truth of others...or has it?

Let us address for a moment the true reality. You are an infinite being, you are a creator, and you have an unlimited supply of energy to create whatever reality you choose. The people that are around you, be it your family, friends or strangers, these are your physical "brothers and sisters" but in actuality are YOU. We mean this in the sense that you are made of precisely the same energy, but also in the sense that you ARE the same Source expressing as individual identities – only appearing to be separate based on your individual perspectives. You are an infinite being that cannot die and cannot be destroyed in your most basic form. This is the Truth of who you are. Now let us address this illusion that the Ego Self has created: you are vulnerable, you are weak, and you need protection from everyone and everything. You need your Ego Self to tell you the harsh Truth about others, even though in reality this is your perspective of what others think, and you need your Ego Self to hold your hand through this process or you can't do it alone.

Well, this seems awfully strange. This Ego Self seems to be the complete opposite of what is true about you. This Ego Self wants you to relate to fear, disease and separation so that you cannot and will not ever embrace your power. The Ego Self so desperately does not want you to release its mastery over you, so much so, that the Ego Self will keep you attached and connected only to your physical body. The Ego Self will make you think that you are your body, that you are tied to this Earth merely as a physical body walking around stuck in a world out of your control. What is the most perfect way for this Ego Self to keep you tied to your body in such a way? It is illness, of course. What better way is there to make you think that you are a helpless body swaying in the ocean, being dragged this way and that way by the current? The Ego Self loves to harbor thoughts that lead to illness, that lead your physical body to break down and ultimately lead to death, because it is this impending death that truly dooms you. You spend so long being fearful of death thinking, "Oh no, I have so much to do before this impending dooms day. This day that I will cease to be. I only have one life to live, so I must hurry and I must do precisely what society tells me deems me to be a success in this life, and I MUST do it at the rate that society deems acceptable." You spend so much time focusing on that END result of death that you forget to truly enjoy the ride. The Ego Self loves to trap you into this cycle; it loves to keep you blind of the truth: that you cannot be sick unless you choose, and you do not die unless you choose. A truly enlightened physical being consciously chooses the time of their death, death does not choose them. You would do very well to remember this.

And so we say that this Ego Self has one true agenda at heart: to keep you blind of the truth of who you truly are. It traps you in the illusions of illness, despair and ultimate pending death, so that you fail to see the truth of who you are. By keeping you tied solely to your physical aspect, until your untimely death, the Ego Self has served its function well in preventing you from seeing the light and awakening to who you truly are. Of course, this is of no concern, dearest one – for as you will learn, this is all as it was meant to be and is essential for an authentic experience of growth and expansion!

Now, allow us to continue with our explanation of detecting the difference between Ego Self and Authentic Self operation. To best understand the difference that exists between the Ego Self and the Authentic Self, it is important to pay attention to your Emotional Indicator. Doing so will allow you to identify your emotions and then determine whether you are being directed by Authentic Self or by Ego Self. When your emotions indicate Joy and happiness and your thoughts create an overall feeling of contentment, we would say that you are operating as Authentic Self. On the other hand, when you have thoughts that trigger emotional responses such as hate, anger, resentment or jealousy, these emotions are an indication that you are being directed by the Ego Self. It is simpler understood that when you feel emotions that are not derivative of Love, Peace and Joy, which is the natural emotional state when being directed by Authentic Self, then you are receiving guidance from the Ego Self. However, please note, this does not need to be a detrimental occurrence. When this occurs and when these emotions begin to fester, you need only acknowledge that you must shift your Alignment. You need only affirm that you must shift your attention to thoughts of Love, Joy, and Peace and in performing this shift, you will realign Self. That is all that need be done! You do not need to wallow, and you do not need to feel guilt; you simply need to realign Self.

How can you tell the difference? By following what feels right to you! If your thoughts ring Truth to you, if they resonate with you and make your heart sing, embrace them! If your thoughts drum up insecurities, feelings of fear, resentment or anger, recognize them for what they are and choose the alternative. It is really that simple. For now we will leave this subject and move onto an understanding of how to eliminate the Ego Self's hold on you.

LESSON 6
ELIMINATING THE EGO SELF

To best understand what we mean by "eliminate the Ego Self's hold on you," we must first discuss why it is that the Ego Self has a hold on you. Until you acknowledge that you are allowing this devil to control you, you will not fully assume the role of master and silence this illusion once and for all. To best understand the Ego Self, we must return again to the beginning – to when the separation occurred. This idea that you could be separate from your brothers and sisters and ultimately from Source is what caused your mind to split from Authentic Self Alignment. This belief that you had to protect and defend your own needs against the very essence of that which you are is what caused you to forget your power. The vibrational descent of truly becoming physical was a very monumental decision and one that was not taken lightly. It was a decision to leave comfort, to leave home and to ultimately take a chance on our ability to trust in our power and our connection to all life in the Universes. Although we always had this knowing assessable to us, we found the needs of the physical plane to be overbearing and exhausting. We found the stresses of the physical body to be too much to bear, and so we allowed this concept of fear to fester. Of course, there is much more to the story that will be discussed at another time, but for now this understanding is sufficient. Our dear brothers and sisters, it is now time to overcome this fear, which we allowed to overtake us so long ago. It is time to embrace your power and remember that we are the Masters, that we will not be tamed by our creations; we will rise above them and embrace who we are. This of course may not be perceived as easy; for it were, the world would be in a much different place.

We will now discuss the path that must be taken to overcome this hold that the Ego Self has on you. Firstly, it must be embraced and fully accepted that you are the one who chooses your fate. You are the one who chooses every thought and every emotion you allow to fester. Regardless of what has happened to you in your life, we will always say the same thing: it was by your attraction and request that these situations happened into your life. As difficult as that may be to hear, it is the truth. Secondly, you must dedicate your Self, knowing that this may not be perceived as easy. Know that there may be difficult information and unpleasant data, which you have accumulated throughout your life that will be drummed up to the surface for no other purpose than to be mastered and overcome. All thoughts – and we mean ALL thoughts – are valid. If they feel limiting – if they pain you – they are coming to the surface to be addressed. Lastly, we ask that you hide nothing. That you hide nothing from your Self and from your Family of Light and that you allow us to assist you in transmuting everything that no longer serves you. This may not be perceived as easy, but it will be so rewarding.

And so we say to you now, there is much to be learned, processed and understood. You must be open, you must be perceptive, and you must be willing to leave any and all limitations and inhibitions at the door. Step off the ledge – hold nothing back – and you will be generously rewarded!

To continue with this lesson, we will now delve further into the Ego Self illusion. What have we learned of the Ego Self thus far? We have learned that it is a creation of the mind, a creation of your doing that allows you to operate without the instruction of Higher Self. As it is your creation, yours to do with as you choose, you can decide at any moment to cast this Ego Self creation aside and operate solely as Authentic Self. Now, in saying this, let us remind you that this process is not as simple as it may sound. The fact is, these understandings seem so straightforward and yet are so complex at the same time. Today, you must come to understand the intricacy with which the Ego Self creation has engrained itself into your existence. Please note that we do not wish to make you feel as though you have failed at anything or as though you have allowed your Self to be taken in by an actual devil. Understand that when we address these things, we are not saying that the Ego Self is real at all – as this "devil" does not exist beyond the illusions of the physical world. However, for the understandings that must be achieved and for the mind to grasp what we are teaching you, you must come to see the Ego Self as a separate entity from the True You – a pure illusion of the physical world that is, in reality, nothing at all. It is your created illusion and your creation to do with as you choose. So please always remember first and foremost, this is not an infinite indestructible creation – it is simply a choice.

We draw your attention to your birth, to the moment you entered into this physical world. When you left your true home, you were firm in your understandings, you were concrete in your knowings, but you made a choice – a choice to descend. This choice brought with it many challenging concepts for you, the most trying being starting from scratch. You would incarnate having the connection to Authentic Self always available to you, but you would also incarnate with an infantile mind that would allow for a disconnect of Self to be made available. Allow us to explain what we mean by this. When you are born Authentic Self is readily available to you, but so is the opportunity for a disconnected Self. You are born with the knowing of who you truly are; however, you are also born without the necessary data or physical training required to remain in Authentic Self Alignment from your new vantage point. Being physical is a very different and unique experience every time you emerge and by your own choice, you were plunged into this world. Plunged into a new reality feeling intense collective energies of separation and fear – initiating the programming process of Self. This is where your parents or guardians came in. Your guardians were your "handlers" in the physical world. (Please do not be concerned if you were adopted or abandoned as a child, as this was the journey that was deemed the best route for your soul expansion.) At the moment you entered the world and you were greeted by your handlers, your journey in the physical began. You came into the world having access to Authentic Self at all times, but the energies that surrounded you encompassed you. The amassed vibrations of the Collective Consciousness, of the people around you and of your very guardians were much stronger than you could have anticipated. Though you were born with the potential for perfect Self Alignment, the energies very quickly and very easily overcame you, forcing you and your defense mechanism into a state of panic. Everything was so different and a complete shock for Self, and so began the disconnect from Authentic Self Alignment.

Depending on the path assigned for your physical journey, you may have grown up in a home were Authentic Self Alignment and Joy were embraced, or alternatively, you may have grown up in a home were fear reigned supreme. It matters not what your path was, neither is better or worse. Both routes, and ultimately the million different possibilities that existed within these routes, are equally necessary and equally important in propelling each soul into the experiences they longed and desired to partake in. And so regardless of the childhood upbringing you had, regardless of what type of nurturing environment you were presented with, you were all lead here. Here together, to this very same point in time.

So where is it that we are now? Where is it exactly that you find your Self now? As a result of which ever childhood you chose, regardless of how perfect it could have appeared, you have been programmed with erroneous data from your guardians and society. You have come to know things that do not serve you; you have come to believe things that do not serve you. And so you may ask, "Where does Ego Self play into all this"? Well, every thought of separation, every "bad" memory and every "bad" experience in your past, were all experiences collected while you were misaligned as Self and while you were operating as Ego Self. There isn't a single experience that exists in your mind that is fear based, that was not collected during Self misalignment. And so you may say, "What about these experiences? They are traumatic experiences that happened to me that I did not ask for and that I did not want." First let us say, we greatly sympathize with your sufferings. We would never wish that upon anyone; however, we would also never wish to take that experience from you. Every experience, whether perceived as good or bad, is an essential part of your soul's growth. It may be difficult to hear this, but it will only make you stronger; it will only help propel you toward your purpose and onto your desired path in this life.

We understand that for those who have come from situations of abuse, this concept can be difficult to comprehend, but we assure you this was the path chosen for Self. These specific experiences were necessary. Although this may be difficult to understand at this point in time, soon you will come to accept everything that has happened to you. You will accept it as part of a necessary plan, and you will acknowledge all roles within these experiences as being essential. You will look at all involved with compassion and understanding. Eventually, you will get to a place where these experiences no longer feed negativity and, instead, give you valuable insights into that which you now choose to attract. Remember, these experiences are neither good nor bad, they are simply points of attraction.

In closing, allow us now to return back to this understanding of operating as Ego Self. Whenever you experienced any version of misery, jealously, hatred, anger, any form of fear or anything contrary to love and Joy, this was collected and experienced through Ego Self. But remember, this in itself was neither good nor bad. The Ego Self is not something to fear or throw stones at. This creation was a very valuable tool that taught you who you truly are and how you truly wish to operate, which is out of love and Joy. This creation may have been essential, but no one wants to feel pain and no one wants to feel uncomfortable, so who in their right mind would want to continue to operate as Ego Self knowing all this? Even though you will vow now to eradicate this Ego Self, you must be patient and allow your Self the necessary time to do this correctly. You must remember that when we look at the hold that the Ego Self has on you, we must look so with compassionate eyes. We must look so with a sympathetic understanding that this Ego Self was with you at the very beginning and has operated beside you for so many years, and so this process may take time. Please be easy on your Self, and remember this is not an overnight method. There are many streams of data, many beliefs to be reprogrammed, but it will be done, and you will succeed. Do not fear this process of bringing that which is hidden in the darkness into the light of truth. Embrace it with open arms, and allow this process to be as painless as possible. Very good today, friend. We will pick up in the next lesson furthering your understandings on the eradication of the Ego Self.

LESSON 7
AUTHENTIC SELF ALIGNMENT

Today we will waste no time with our most important goal of eradicating the Ego Self. We will start this message by affirming that we will no longer serve this Ego Self by drawing our attention to it. In this moment, the Ego Self exists for you no longer, and you will operate as Authentic Self only. Let us set the intention together that you wish for Authentic Self Alignment, and this will be our primary goal at all times. We will briefly continue to discuss this Ego Concept from a point of non-attachment and for observational purposes, strictly for further knowledge. Today, we are going to continue a previous discussion on the components of Self. As we have expressed, Authentic Self is comprised of the Body, Mind and Soul (or Higher Self) working in perfect Alignment and in perfect procession. This is our goal. Our goal is total Authentic Self Alignment, free of past data and limiting energetic blocks, and this is where your thoughts must remain at all times. Allow us now to return to the beginning of these understandings, the beginning where it was explained that the Ego Self was a creation of the mind, simply so that the experience of separation could occur. This is what we would like to elaborate on now.

When we say that the creation of the Ego Self was of the mind, it is better understood that the creation of the Ego Self was of Higher Self. This may seem such a strange concept, but let us stop and identify who you truly are. You are Higher Self, and you are not your body or your mind. You are an individualized aspect known as "Insert your name here" and you are Higher Self expressing through this individualized aspect for growth and expansion. You are not defined by your personality or individualized aspect, as the True You is not confined to physicality. In the same respect, the individualized aspect that is "You," the personality, cannot exist without Higher Self. Therefore, it is best to remember that "You" are Self. You are an integration of Body, Mind and Soul. And so when we refer to the Ego Self as being a creation of Higher Self, let us address the concept from this vantage point.

Higher Self created the aspect known as "Self" for expansion and growth. Self was essential so that growth could occur from the experience of both the light and the dark – the good and the bad. Thus allowing the opportunity for a test of remembrance, brute strength and knowing that would ultimately result in realignment. In order for this test to be authentic, in order for a true individualized personality to be created for growth, it was essential that data was collected outside of the parameters of an Authentic Self connection. From this understanding sprang forth the necessity for the Ego Self. Yes, the Ego Self was created as a result of a disengaged Self, which ultimately sprang forth from the defense mechanisms and a need to protect oneself against all others. BUT this is not to say that this was not the plan from the beginning.

The Ego Self was a necessary creation, and although this is often difficult to understand, this concept will be discussed in further detail throughout these lessons. For you must always remember that the Earth was created as a school, a means by which you would grow and expand. And true growth and expansion would not be a possibility without an authentic testing ground. And so the Ego Self came to be so that you could fully immerse your Self in the illusion of duality – in perceived separation and the great battle between light and dark, good and bad and opposites in opposition. And by being immerse in this created illusion, you would find your way home.

The Ego Self was a required creation for many reasons. The first being that it was an absolute necessity for the illusion of duality to exist, to allow the opportunity for authentic free will choices to be made. Secondly, the Ego Self was a necessary creation simply because you needed something to blame. You needed a scape goat to blame for all that mankind does. Instead of taking accountability, which is an approach derived from a developed level of consciousness, you were meant to blame one another and the "devil" within them for all the bad things in this world. Such was the purpose for the battle between light and dark and the necessary continuation of a perceived separation. For without this perceived separation, there could be no real experience of duality and therefore no true growth and expansion. And so we deemed this to be the best means by which one could learn and grow, and out of the veiled darkness of unseen Truths, emerge into the light. A created testing grounds, produced and fashioned from our intention that it be so – for the mere thrill of growth and expansion!

Please remember, for authentic growth and expansion, it had to be this way. The creation of the Ego Self was a necessary part of the experience so that your mind could collect data both of the darkness and of the light – of the truths and of the unseen truths. These experiences that were collected while under the control of Ego Self were absolutely vital. This time of Ego Self-control not only created experiences that resulted in who you are today, it also allowed your mind true data that would be in need of reprogramming. Such was the purpose of the physical world school experience – generated and maintained by authentic testing grounds. From this perspective, one can understand that in order to achieve the desired effect of overcoming the darkness, one must first be presented with the darkness. The test had to be authentic. And so from this perspective we can see why the creation of Ego Self was so very essential. We can see that all that exists of the perceived "darkness" IS the light and in reality our own creation for growth and expansion! There is no separation; there is but one.

We must now address what plagues many when we reach this point of understandings. This sense of "Who am I?" You are the Soul – Higher Self having a physical experience. You are not the physical or mental aspects of Self – you are Higher Self. We will elaborate on this further. The body is the means by which you exist physically, the means by which you have form. The body is the communication device, the way you interact with other incarnated beings and the means by which you collect data. The mind is your operating system. The mind's sole purpose is to operate the current version of Self. The mind houses a compilation of data from Ego Self Alignment and Higher Self Alignment. It is this compilation of data that makes up your current version of Self. When you are operating as Ego Self, the data appears to be "bad" or "negative," and when you are operating as Authentic Self, your experiences appear to be Joyous and are perceived as "good" data. Therefore, when we address the current make up of data being processed by your mind, it is clear that your current version of Self will be a mash up of both perceived negative and positive data.

On one hand, we have this data that was collected purely for physical growth and expansion, which you might call negative data, and on the other hand, we have data that was for the purpose of Self-Realization. Let us explain further. The data that is perceived as being negative is a collection of all perceived "bad" experiences; but in truth, this data is in fact not bad at all. It is neither good nor bad. It was a point of attraction for you so that you would learn from it and at a later time overcome said data, when you were ready. Hence, fully engaging your Self in the test of physicality – the rewarding experience of overcoming the illusion of duality. On the flip side, the Joyous moments are moments of Self-Realization where you welcome the creative being that you are, sense your oneness with All That Is and fully embrace your connectedness as Authentic Self. Both of these moments are equally important, and in reality both are essential to overall growth and expansion for Higher Self.

Now we will discuss the process by which the mind will begin to operate the upgraded 2.0 version of Self or, essentially, how the mind will operate the Authentic version of Self. You are operating a version of Self that is a combination of both Ego Self programming and Authentic Self programming. However, as we indicated in the beginning, we are no longer acknowledging that there is an Ego Self, so let us give a new name to this programming. We will call this your limiting programming. This was data that was collected when you were influenced by the often challenging aspects of human existence and by the energies of society and the Collective Consciousness. Where you collected data that was not of your own true nature, which was evident all around you in your experiences. We are not saying that you do not have to take accountability for these energies, because you allowed them of course, but as we have said, these energies were part of the plan, so to speak. This limiting programming was essential for growth and expansion.

Let us move forward declaring that you only have your limiting programming and your Authentic Self programming. From this new perspective, we will continue. As we have indicated previously, it is essential that we reprogram the current version of Self so that you can achieve TOTAL Authentic Self Alignment and return to your former glory as a Joyous being. The only way to achieve this is through the receiving of knowing via Authentic Self Alignment. During this Alignment, the mind is able to download data from Higher Self that reprograms the previously collected limiting programing and resulting limiting beliefs. This data must be downloaded so that the previous thought patterns and limiting beliefs that once held you, are no longer relevant. This is not to say that this limiting belief data will not continue to exist in your mental data bank, but what we are saying is that this data will no longer hold power over you. It will exist as one with all collected data, but the majority data will shift from limitations to infinite possibilities, and this limiting programming will cease to exist in your current experience.

In closing, let us now recap what we have learned. All data that is in your mind is essential. All data is part of the plan for growth and expansion. You are operating a current version of Self that is a blend of data from limiting programming and Higher Self programming via Authentic Self Alignment. Moving forward, you are now going to focus on the understanding that all data that is perceived as "negative" was essential so that you could achieve desired growth and expansion. ALL data was necessary. And so moving forward, we will not say that any data or experience was good or bad – we will say that ALL was essential and offers excellent potential for growth when properly analyzed. This is where we will venture in the next lessons. We will discuss how to analyze past experiences to detect the value within them and in doing so determine what limiting beliefs can be reprogrammed through said observation.

CHAPTER 2
OVERCOMING FEAR

CHAPTER 2
INTRODUCTION

We are most pleased with your progress thus far, but know, dearest brothers and sisters, that moving forward there is much work to be done. In the upcoming lessons you will find your Self face to face with your greatest fears, and we assure you these lessons will require immense focus and mental discipline if you wish to proceed whole heartedly onto Chapter 3. Please remember that through this process, these lessons need only be as painful or as Joyous as you allow them to be. If you wish to sail through your limiting belief reprograming quickly and efficiently, you need only set the intention to do so. But know this, brothers and sisters, an empty intention and an empty promise is useless and will reap rewards that reflect contradiction. Know that if you set intentions in an attempt to fool your Self or the Universe, it most certainly will not be done. Do not lie to your Self or to us in the moments when you may feel resistance or great frustration and say that you have done all that you could and the fault is not yours. This would be a great injustice to your power. No, we tell you now, in these moments when you may falter, when you may encounter great resistance, have no fear, and move forward acknowledging the work to be done and set your intentions accordingly. Do not allow fear to rule you at any moment in time, and ensure that you are the master of your mind.

Before we begin, we wish to remind you that you need not pay so much attention to the superficial meaning of the scenarios presented in these upcoming lessons. When we begin to discuss experiences and events that have manifested in the lives of many Lightworkers, know that your manifested situations may have occurred precisely the same or slightly different. However, know that the intention of our explanation of these situations is to show you examples of how your thoughts could have manifested onto the physical plane. Know that no two experiences will be alike, and moving forward, these lessons are not only fundamental to your own reprogramming, but also contain essential knowledge to ultimately assist you in the healing of others. You must fully understand and grasp the concepts discussed, so that you may no longer remain shackled to your limiting beliefs, and you can walk fearlessly into the new world creating your Heaven on Earth. We applaud you for your progress thus far, and we are pleased to take this next step of the journey with you. As always, we will remain beside you through this process – now and forever. Love and Light.

LESSON 8
LIMITING BELIEFS

W e will begin Lesson 8 – and this most important chapter – with a very brief recap. So that we are all on the same page, we will ensure that you have absorbed what must be absorbed for the next set of intentions in these lessons. By now you fully understand your purpose for incarnation. You understand that you came forth with the sole purpose of growth and expansion, that you are a Divine Creator, and that you have orchestrated all of your experiences and circumstances so that you may achieve said growth and expansion. You understand your role, and you embrace and appreciate that you have a Global Purpose in addition to your Personal Purpose, which is prodding at you to fulfill a specific assignment. Clarification on your complete assignment is where we would like to begin our discussion today.

We will begin by stating the obvious: as growth seeking beings, your happiness and your Joy cannot exist with your sole focus being only on your global purpose. What type of true growth and expansion can occur from only one aspect of your existence? No, to be well-rounded, your growth and expansion must come forth from all aspects of your existence, and this includes your personal purpose. For many, their personal purposes include things such as having children, having a spouse, etc., but can range to other extremes such as being a rock star, a drug addict and so forth. It may seem so bizarre to say that these are examples of purposes, but the fact of the matter is, it is these personal purposes that allow us to achieve personal level growth and expansion for our soul. We will explain further. The global purpose that we have discussed is an intention that was set forth before incarnation. An intention to assist the world in the Ascension process. This in itself offers wonderful potential for growth and expansion, but you would not have agreed to come back had it not offered additional well-rounded growth and expansion that you desired. Now in saying this, let us express that it was not like you said, "Well, what is in it for me?" To the contrary, you were very eager to provide your services, but you were likewise enthusiastic to achieve your own personal growth and expansion, through physical experiences you desired to have outside of your global purpose. And so when we say your personal purpose is equally as essential to overall growth and expansion, this is what we mean: you came forth equally eager to fulfill both purposes – to achieve growth and expansion on all levels of your being, not merely one aspect.

So let us address this concept of growth and expansion further. Let us use an example:

When one chooses to have a family for growth and expansion, what is it that can be achieved by such an experience? For many, in past lives you were deprived of the experience of such a personal purpose, as your intention for physical world existence was to serve the greater good. We will explain this further. In past lives, there were many that incarnated to serve the purpose of creating legacies throughout human history. They were to be the knowledge keepers, the crusaders of the light, if you will, to ensure that knowledge was not lost through the ages. And so in these times you did not come forth with the same personal purposes as you might have in this life. When this life came to be, you made a very strict list and a non-negotiable set of requirements that were essential for your own personal growth and expansion, i.e. many chose families, as they were not able to fully embrace this experience in past lives; some chose fame as they were considered outcasts in past lives; others chose trauma based lives so that their soul could have the challenge of overcoming this obstacle and provide a wonderful and much needed example for all. Really, it does not matter which path was chosen as ALL are equally important, and each present their own "difficulties." We will not delve into these perceived difficulties because as we have learned in previous lessons, all is a gift for growth and expansion, and ALL is necessary.

When we address these personal purposes, we do so that you always remember that you came forth to serve your global purpose, as well as your personal purpose. You must never lose sight of this fact. Your reason for existing on the physical plane is not only to serve others, it is to serve your own desire for growth and expansion first. It is your primary focus to find your Joy and your happiness, and in doing so assist the world in so many ways, above and beyond your global purpose. And so as we begin this journey, this journey of fully remembering who you are and eliminating the limiting beliefs that no longer serve you, keep all priorities in mind.

Move forward with the knowing that you are meant to delve into any and all experiences you desire to have, and you are not simply meant to dedicate all that you do to helping others. This will not result in balance and a well-rounded experience of growth and expansion. Frankly, by operating in this manner, you will find only resistance and dismay, as an unhappy Lightworker is an unproductive Lightworker. Please friends, beautiful brothers and sisters, learn to find your Joy in all aspects of your life, and DO NOT EVER forget about your personal purposes in the process of chasing your global dreams. Remember to focus as much time on the limiting beliefs associated with your personal purpose as you do your global purpose – for both aspects are essential to your journey.

With this understanding in mind at all times, we will recommence with Lesson 8. In this lesson we will begin the process of identifying and eliminating beliefs that no longer serve you. Our primary intention for this chapter is to allow you to truly see the limiting programming that has led to your many limiting beliefs and in doing so, allow you to overcome the illusion of physical world duality. Understand that these beliefs that you hold keep you trapped in the illusions of separation, powerlessness and opposites in opposition, and they ensure that you are unable to ascend to a level of consciousness that allows you to achieve all that you desire. In understanding and overcoming all limiting beliefs through reprogramming, you will achieve a state of mind where this limiting programming is no longer the dominant thought, and you will realize a state of peace and Joy unlike anything you have ever known in this life time.

We will begin this process of reprogramming by examining past experiences, from an observational viewpoint only, so that we may recognize the repeated patterns and ultimately the limiting beliefs within your manifested situations. When we say we will do so from an observational approach, let us explain what we mean. When we delve into past experiences, we must do so with an understanding that the past merely provides data to assist us in our current experience. As awakened beings, we fully recognize that past events were for growth and expansion and only exist in a chronological order to assist us on our path. These past events are not to be lingered upon, they are ONLY to serve you in determining what new experiences you would like to produce in your current experience. We will stress that discussing these limiting beliefs is not an excuse to fester emotions and re-launch an Ego Self. You of course can do this at any time that you choose, but you are an awakened being, and you will not choose the path of destruction. You will choose to keep Authentic Self aligned and bring to the light of truth all that does not serve you. Please remember as we discuss these things that you created them for your own growth and expansion; you created these experiences to create the individualized personality that is your physical aspect. You created these experiences so that you could ultimately overcome them – so let us do that together now!

When we discuss this concept of a limiting belief, what exactly is meant? A limiting belief is limiting programming received by society or the collective consciousness that has resulted in you building beliefs that limit the power of Self. When we say "building," we mean precisely what is implied. It is not a situation where you one time received data saying that you were "controlled by circumstances" and then all of a sudden you forgot that you hold the power to create your reality. No, this is most certainly not the case. You received copious amounts of similar data that contributed and essentially built these limiting beliefs. In this respect, please understand that this copious amount of data will have to be counteracted with a sufficient amount of reprogramming data so that a new belief and a new perspective can be formed. During this process it may seem like we are repeating thoughts and concepts, but remember we must achieve the desired overriding data to operate Self 2.0 effectively. We will begin the next lesson by discussing the Core Limiting Beliefs that you have acquired throughout your time on the physical plane. This will include past life beliefs, as well as current life beliefs.

During this process, there will be data that comes to the surface for transmutation. There will be data that offers resistance within you, but do not run and hide; instead, let us face it together. It is only through recognizing the shift from Authentic Self Alignment and acknowledging that there is clarity to be received that you can remove your fear from these moments that you perceive despair. These moments where you wonder, "Have I taken two steps back?" In actuality, these moments are wonderful opportunities for growth and expansion and are essential to the collection of the necessary data to overcome the limiting beliefs that resulted in the current situation you find your Self in. So please do not allow your Self to become miss aligned unnecessarily. When you feel these emotions, it is time to smile because you have now been presented with a limiting belief to Recognize, Analyze and Re-Strategize. This is progress and propels you on your path!

LESSON 9
SELF WORTH

Today we will begin one of numerous lessons on limiting beliefs and the Three Steps of Realization: Recognize, Analyze and Re-Strategize. The time spent on these lessons may be considered by some to be a period of difficulty, but how you choose to receive these lessons is up to you. Remember, you do not have to permit these lessons to be painful or to be a burden. You can choose for this to be a Joyous experience of Self-cleansing and Self-Realization. The choice is yours.

Today, we are going to begin with a limiting belief that affects the majority – Self-Worth. This is a dominant block for Lightworkers, as it is in your nature to want to assist. We will proceed to Recognize how this Core Limiting Belief came to be and allow you to identify the pattern this belief has created throughout your life. We will then proceed to Analyze what effect this belief is having on your current experiences, and lastly, we will begin to Re-Strategize, so that we may work toward the ultimate goal of transmutation. When we say "Self-Worth" what do we mean? We mean the value you place on your existence. We mean the value you place on taking care of you, of course, but we truly mean the value you give your own life. For many people, they spend so long and so many hours taking care of others that they do not value their own Self enough to recognize that they need care as well. Although we do not argue that taking care of others can be very rewarding, at the end of the day if you do not take care of you, who will? And so let us discuss why this occurs, and where this began as a pattern.

One of the dominant similarities between Lightworkers is that the vast majority of you were born into society feeling different. Although many may have felt love and appreciation from some physical family members, many of you overall felt alone and unappreciated. We will not delve into why this experience was essential, but we will say that there was of course a reason why you chose this experience. And so many of you grew up feeling as though you were "adopted," without any real friends and as though you were an outcast or alienated because of your perceived "weirdness." You may have socialized with others, but generally the interactions were superficial and with no true connection. This is not to say that along your path there weren't fellow Lightworkers that incarnated with you, to assist both of you on your journeys. This could have been a friend that felt more like a sibling that you had known for years. Perhaps this friend was not a physical human at all; perhaps it was a pet of some sort. It does not matter. The fact is you would have found some sort of companion to make the days a little easier. From this perspective of loneliness and alienation sprang the beginning of your manifested Self-Worth issues.

Now remember, these were merely the physical world "situations" that began to manifest showing the underlying

Self-Worth issues. We will explain this further. All things that exist on the physical plane must first spring forth from the mind. This is the case for EVERYTHING. The physical plane is merely a mirror of the mental plane and, ultimately, the spiritual plane. So, what does this suggest then? This suggests that these physical world situations, which are "perceived" to be the beginning of your Self-Worth issues, were not really the beginning of your Self-Worth issues at all. So let us take this back further then, to when you were born. As we have expressed before, all Lightworkers come forth with both personal and global purposes. Lightworkers are very unique from other souls as a result of this global purpose. This strong pre-birth intention to desire an Authentic Self connection, due to your global purpose, is very evident from the moment you enter through the birth cannel. As a result, this can cause periods of miss alignment to be extremely difficult for you. You spend your days with a strong built-in beacon telling you to align your Self and start working on your global purpose, and yet you are thrown into a world overwhelmed by fear based energies and limiting beliefs. Due to this strong pre-birth intention, many Lightworkers find great struggle in the world. You are a Master and choosing to collect data that is different and opposite from your true nature is very challenging, as your knowing of the truths is very dominant. And so many of you then spend your years feeling as though you are so out of place and so very different, ALL as a result of this miss aligned Self. Let us explain further.

If all form evolves from the mental plane and manifests onto the physical plane as a mirrored image, this would mean that your sense of displacement, your sense of feeling different due to the constant struggle to fit into the "Ego Self" construct, would have created great turmoil and powerful emotions within you. As a result, this same vibration would then, via the Law of Attraction, mirror this sense of displacement into your physical situations. This expressed itself as alienation with peers, with family, or with society in general. This expressed itself as a struggle to fit into the mold society deemed acceptable. Understand, for the majority of society this "Ego Self" construct feels normal and like second nature, but for you – a Lightworker – it is indeed a struggle. So where they would feel completely comfortable and at home, you would feel awkward and out of place, beginning on the mental plane and then mirroring onto the physical plane. Simply put, the data that you began to collect in mass quantities the moment you were born was so very contrasting to your built-in programming urging you to exist in Authentic Self Alignment to fulfill your global purpose. This great contrast caused such discomfort and a significant rift in the thoughts produced, resulting in the physical manifestation of various situations and experiences that mirrored this mental contrast in a tangible form. Hence, creating physical experiences that created your perceived Self-Worth issues.

From this perspective, let us now discuss how this created a limiting belief that patterned throughout your life. For most Lightworkers, this pattern continues for many, many years, but if addressed early on, it can be understood and overcome quickly and efficiently. We know that this pattern is created out of the limiting belief that begins with a struggle of a miss aligned Self. Now, let us discuss how exactly this pattern is created. In the beginning, the core issue was a miss aligned Self, and as this mirrored onto the physical plane as manifested situations, more and more data was collected. More and more physical world data came forth displaying this mental conflict, as you were emotionally tied to this feeling of disconnect. As this data collected, you began to feel stranger and more alienated. From this concept sprang very deep and very real Self-Worth issues. As you spent much of your childhood feeling as though you were the outcast, it is of course no wonder that you would then begin to feel that you were the weird one, the unimportant one, and the one that did not belong. You began to feel as though you should try to fit in and assimilate, and for the many who continuously try this route, it often leads to numerous experiences of self-destruction through alcohol, drugs and pain. This is not your true nature, but as a result of the overwhelming pressure to assimilate, your sense of displacement in society only continues to grow and Self-Worth only continues to disintegrate.

Let us now discuss how this Self-Worth concept relates to low Self-Worth as a Lightworker. As you grew, you often felt as though you were the strange one. You felt out of place and believed that all others were the normal ones and that their "normal" mindsets and way of life represented what was meant to be achieved. You spent your time trying to fit in and be like them, regardless of the struggle it may have caused you. Your Self-Worth plummeted as you began to feel as though the "you" inside, your values and knowing, was not of importance. You began to believe that the knowing that prodded you was strange and not of significance. You began at a very young age to devalue how you feel and what you know, simply because it would not be accepted by others.

Your Self-Worth issues run so deep that by the time you discover who you really are, it is engrained within you to worry so much about what other people think. You then confuse helping others with your own false data of fearing that people will be upset with you if you say what you really think and express what you truly want to do. Many Lightworkers create a pattern of "helping" because they feel that they must and do not realize that these efforts are in fact tainted with fear based energy. Any time that you feel you are tired, hungry, need a break, need to relax and you then decide to help another instead, this is tainted with fear based energy. Now let us explain, we are not devaluing your assistance of others, but what we are trying to stress is that anytime you offer assistance with the true desire of really wanting to do something for your Self, your intention will not be pure as it is laced with a sense of Self-Sacrifice. It is this concept of Self-Sacrifice that we will move onto in the next lesson, as it represents a central theme and limiting belief for Lightworkers.

LESSON 10
SELF SACRIFICE

We will embark upon Lesson 10 utilizing the same method as the previous lesson. We will Recognize the Core Limiting Belief and the pattern presented, Analyze how it has manifested into your current experiences and begin to Re-Strategize, so that we may recommence the process of transmutation. Today, we are going to discuss the limiting belief of Self-Sacrifice, but we will do so from a unique perspective, as we will also touch upon Self-Sacrifice in relation to the past lives you have experienced. What do we mean by Self-Sacrifice? This is a process by which you choose to sacrifice the needs and wants of Self in order to deliver the needs and wants of another. We will also refer to this Self-Sacrifice in the literal sense of sacrificing the existence of Self in order to assist the greater good.

We will begin with this understanding of sacrifice in past lives. For many of you, you have already begun to vaguely remember situations that occurred in past lives. Although you may not consciously remember who or what role you were playing, you will have the strangest fears that seem to come out of nowhere, from no logical point of origin. These fears are often times related to your past life experiences. Let us use The Channel, Amanda, as an example.

In a past life, the Higher Self of Amanda existed as, what one from a modern perspective would refer to as, a "witch." This word is of course taken greatly out of context, and it is better understood that she was a healer. She worked very closely with nature and the elements and was a master of utilizing the natural world to serve many purposes – such as physical healing and element manipulation for crop growth. She was very powerful and revered, but as was her intention, the time came when the ways of her community resulted in a misunderstanding of her abilities and she was persecuted for "perceived" wrong doings. During this experience, "Amanda" was hung from a tree and was left to watch her family as they witnessed her passing. As Amanda experienced this past life during a lucid dreaming experience, this was of course a very difficult moment for her to process.

In this moment, she completely felt the emotions of this past aspect as her soul departed the physical body. Although many would say, "What a terrible thing to want to see," this experience provided many useful tools and data to assist Amanda in her current experience. Firstly, what was determined during this regression was a validation of her knowing of being hung in a previous life, as well as a reasoning for her current fear of enclosures around her neck. What was also understood was her great sadness as a result of leaving her family in that life; but more importantly, what she realized was that she was feeling as though she would have to sacrifice her family in her current experience as well. We do not mean this necessarily in the sense that she thought she was going to die or that her family was. What we mean is that her mind, due to these past energetic imprints, was fearful that she was going to have to focus solely on her global purpose, yet again. Thus, losing the opportunity for the personal purpose of being a mother and wife, which her soul longed for from a growth and expansion perspective. And so seeing this past life allowed Amanda to fully understand why her fear of embracing her global purpose was so strong. She was afraid that if she were to embrace her gifts, something terrible would happen and she would lose her family. Even though she was not sure what these feelings meant and what would happen as a result of these irrational thoughts, the feelings existed nonetheless and presented a limiting belief that prevented her from fully accepting her abilities.

With much practice and dedication, she was able to eliminate this fear. She recognized and accepted that she was not to sacrifice her current physical aspect to serve the purpose of growth and expansion for the collective, as she had done in precious lives. She learned that she was not going to leave her family and deprive her Self of this expansion opportunity. It was her personal purpose in this life to have a family – a permanent non-negotiable personal purpose. This was a very valuable experience for her to see that she was in fact believing that in order to chase her global purpose her family would suffer in some way: be it through embarrassment, some form of harm or a loss of interest on her part as she began to operate more as Authentic Self. All of these fears presented themselves, and through them coming to the surface, she was able to transmute them and recognize that in this life Self is to sacrifice nothing. Self is to have it all!

We will now move on to how this relates to you. You may not have felt this Self-Sacrifice concept as strongly or you may have found it to be precisely the same. You may find that you feel as though you are going to have to give up something to embrace your global purpose. This is not EVER the case. You are here for growth and expansion on a Personal and Global level, and you are not asked to sacrifice anything in this life. Many of you might wonder why you would be asked to sacrifice your experiences in a past life and not this life. This is because in your past lives as an Advocate of Truth, you were there primarily to keep the knowledge alive and to keep the light incarnated throughout your human histories. You came forth in that life knowing that it was not the right time for who you truly are to be revealed and embraced by the masses. You served a most important role in contributing necessary data to the collective that has – and will – continue to assist in these present experiences. But know this – this life is much different. In this life, the world is experiencing a period of Ascension. In this life, a time has come when the collective has grown and expanded to a point where your gifts and abilities will be embraced, and all of the hard work put in by aspects of the past will be rewarded with a present life of complete Joy and bliss. In this life, you will delve whole heartedly into all the experiences you were not able to have in the past. In this life, you will be rewarded for all of your dedication and commitment to the cause. You will literally get to live your Heaven on Earth while in the process assisting others in creating their own version.

Now that an adequate understanding of past life energetic transference has been conveyed, let us move our attention back to the present moment and this concept of Self-Sacrifice.

Due to their Self-Worth issues, as well as contributions from past life fears, many Lightworkers find themselves in a situation of Self-Sacrifice repeatedly throughout their lives. In your past lives, you were incarnated with the intention of a global purpose and with the sole focus of assistance and bringing forth the light that was needed to aid in this present day Ascension. And so this commitment to service has of course carried over into this life. Let us pair this with the Self-Worth issues that have also sprung forth, and you have created quite the limiting belief concoction. As a result, it is highly unlikely given these circumstances that a Lightworker would not find themselves in a situation of low Self-Worth and Self-Sacrifice. So remember, in recognizing this, do not allow any fear based emotions to fester. You have not done anything wrong, and there is nothing to feel guilty about. As you now understand, all occurred as it was meant to for necessary growth and expansion. This process was essential and will make you an optimal example. This is most Joyous to recognize.

From this perspective, one can now understand why you act the way you do. Why you choose to believe that your own care and your own needs come secondary to the needs of others. On the one hand, you have an overbearing need to please and fit in, as a result of low Self-Worth, and on the other hand, you have a continual energetic repetition of this need to serve. This has resulted in you feeling one of two things: that you must assist others as often as they ask because your own needs do not matter, or that even though you would rather be doing something else, you must ignore your own thoughts and assist others with a slight irritation, believing that you have sacrificed something to assist them.

In either case, this does not lead to optimal assistance. We understand at this point many offer a great deal of resistance to this concept of being selfish and taking care of your Self, but we assure you that it is essential that you are cared for FIRST before you care for another. After all, would you tell another that they should ignore their own needs, focus solely on others, and as a result, do away with their own desire for happiness? Of course you would not. You serve your Self and those around you best by ensuring that you, your Self, are acting as the optimal example of vitality and abundance. You perform your healing and teaching functions optimally by first mastering that which you are advocating.

In the same respect, let us also acknowledge what causes perceived separation in the first place: the defense mechanism gone haywire. This mechanism was created to inform you that your body is in need of something. If you continue to ignore these urges from the body, you will cause a disconnect from Authentic Self, and despite how hard you try to realign, you will notice a unsurpassable block come to the surface that will only remove itself with an understanding of why it is there. Remember, brothers and sisters, you are the only one who can truly care for you. If you ignore the needs of the body and you ignore the needs of Self, you will encounter various undesirable manifestations such as illness and physical distress, all of which are a physical symptom of the underlining Self-Sacrifice limiting belief and corresponding thought patterns. So remember, brothers and sisters, it is essential to take care of your Self first, and this begins with the mental plane. If you have continual thoughts of Low Self-Worth or Self-Sacrifice, imagine the ways that this will manifest into your current physical experience.

As the physical plane is a mirror for the mental, there are an infinite number of ways these limiting beliefs could present within your life. Repeated illness is a very common theme, as well as repeated abusive relationships. Whatever manifests shows you that you are not valuing Self. This pattern will not cease until the underlying limiting belief is brought to the surface – to the light – and the fear is removed and the pattern transmuted. We will leave this subject now and move onto the next lesson discussing another Core Limiting Belief.

~You must not be afraid to be you, for being you is the greatest gift you can give to the world.~

LESSON 11
PERFECTIONISM

In today's lesson, we are going to further your understandings of the Core Limiting Beliefs that affect you. Today, we are going to discuss the limiting belief of Perfectionism. Although this may not seem like a relevant hindrance to your role as a Lightworker, we assure you that it is a very vital limiting belief to eradicate. It is a limiting belief that plagues many Lightworkers, even those who believe that they have reached a point free of Ego Self programming. So today, let us discuss this concept of Perfectionism.

We will begin by first saying that we will take the same approach as we have in the previous lessons. We will Recognize the Core Limiting Belief and the pattern that has been presented, we will Analyze how this pattern is affecting your current experience, and we will then Re-Strategize to allow for the transmutation of this limiting belief that does not serve you. When we say Perfectionism, what is it that we mean? We mean Perfectionism in the sense that you do not allow your Self to make perceived "errors," and that you hold your Self to an unrealistic standard that dictates that you are to act as a "supreme" being at all points in time. We assure you that this was not the intention for your incarnation. You were not meant to exist as a "perfect" being, who must act a certain way. Please note that when we say this, we do not mean this in the sense of when you were operating as Ego Self either. What we mean is that you are not meant to act based on the restrictions or beliefs of another, be it a religion or be it following the views of another person or organization, if they do not whole heartedly resonate with you. You are meant to act precisely as you desire and to participate in precisely what your Joy indicates that you would like to partake in.

And so let us explain this further. There are many of you who believe that you should or shouldn't do something or that something is good or bad, simply because another has told you that this is the case. Another has told you things such as eating certain foods is bad, drinking alcohol is bad, watching a frightening or violence based movie is bad or partaking in certain social activities is bad, etc. Well, what we would like you to address today is the Neutrality of all of these circumstances and occurrences. Why is it that these things are perceived as bad; why is it that the opposite of these are perceived as good? And who determines what is considered bad or good? It is certainly not "God" that determines if these things are bad or good because in reality there are no opposites in opposition, and this way of "judgment" thinking was merely a concept created for the dualistic world. And so we ask again, who determines whether these things are bad or good? Whose rules are you following? Your own or someone else's?

We stress today that you remember that it is you who determines what is relevant in your existence. It is you who determines what brings you Joy. And so let us return now to this idea of Perfectionism. This idea that as a Lightworker you must exist a certain way, based on what you believe society has told you is the appropriate way to exist. Let us explain: we are not merely referring to the same concept of limiting data or programming that we referred to in an earlier lesson. We are not only referring to following the guidelines set forth by those that were operating from Ego Self data or of a dual mindset. We are referring to data that you have incorporated into your own experience by others, including those who are on a path of awakening or enlightenment. You view their actions and interpret the data you perceive as data indicating what is to be done or not to be done.

For example:

There is an individual who you believe to be an enlightened being, to be a person in the physical world who has great knowledge and must be in touch with their spiritual side. You admire this person, and you desire the same personal power and personal expansion that you see within them. And so you look at their practices and see that they do not eat meat, they do not drink alcohol, and they do not partake in anything that would be judged a "lower vibration." From this point, you begin to analyze all the things that you do in your life and you begin to say, "If I am doing this, then this must be bad because that person who is advertently good and advanced is not doing these things. Perhaps these things that I am doing are what is preventing me from achieving the same state as this being I admire." You then determine that there are things that you must give up in order to achieve this state of enlightenment or awakening that you desire. With this understanding, we would like to draw your attention back to what we stated in a previous lesson. There is in reality no Joy, but your Joy. There is no other Joy that is right for you, only your own Truths and your own Joy.

Many of you are so trapped within the thrall of the limiting belief of Perfectionism. Yet you do not even recognize the evidence of this, as result of how common place it has become. You are bombarded with information regarding what is considered "success." From birth you are told everything that will supposedly make you happy, and you spend copious amounts of time and dedication working toward achieving these things, only to find that you do not achieve the same state of happiness as others when you obtain what it is that you desired. Again, please note that we are not simply referring to possessions either. We equally refer to achieving mental understandings and levels of obtainable peace. Each of you fight against what it is that feels right to you, as a result of your own Self-Worth and Self-Sacrifice limiting beliefs, and you put all of your effort into someone else's knowing and someone else's path, instead of taking the time to seek your own!

Why is it that this won't work? Well, because each path is unique and each path is personal. What resonates for some will not resonate for all, and although there may be similarities to what individuals' desire, the true intention behind the desire and the experience of what is desired will never be the same. Those of you that spend so much time trying to attain someone else's dream begin a vicious cycle of self-demoralization when you do not achieve this dream or find happiness within said dream.

After your perceived failure, you then find further struggle when you proceed to start all over at achieving this Perfectionism through the same or alternate form. Allow us to explain. As you do not find your Joy within another's dream, your Self-Worth limiting beliefs become more apparent. They are right there informing you that you did not achieve what you desired simply because you were not good enough, not strong enough or wise enough; when in reality, you did not achieve the "success" and Joy you desired because you were trying to follow the path of another instead of your own. In reality, these feelings of dissatisfaction are merely an indication that Self desires something different. Instead of realizing this, many then proceed to move onto plan B of telling themselves to "buck up" and try again OR they proceed to create a new method by which they will attempt to obtain "success" and find their Joy within another's dream. Still they discover the same results of finding little success and absolutely no Joy in the process. The continual search for Perfectionism based on someone else's goals and dreams will always yield the same results. You must come to see that what works for some will not work for all and really there is no global right way – there is no global perfect. You must see this continual search for Perfectionism for what it is and start being gentle with your Self. You must be understanding of your own unique path. You must learn to follow what feels right for you and stop chasing an unobtainable goal.

In saying this, please understand that this idea of Perfectionism – this idea of the type of being you think you are supposed to be – is not based on your own beliefs. It is based on what you have observed to be the "right type" of being. Today, what we would like to stress yet again is that you learn to follow your own Joy. Remove the limitations of right or wrong, good or bad, and begin to dissolve your dualistic mindset. Understand that all there is, is what you desire to have and what you desire to be. Whatever brings you Joy, whatever you desire, is good. And when we say "good," we do not mean in relation to the good vs. bad dual concept, we mean it is unquestionably good and unalterably good, and it is necessary for your path. It is what brings you Joy and it is, what IS for you.

Please remember that during this life when you find that you are drawn to comparing your Self to another – when you are drawn to creating this concept of Perfectionism – you are playing into a limiting belief. Whenever you are trying to attain an image for your Self based on another's actions and perspectives – even though deep down these actions do not resonate with your current path – you are playing into a limiting belief. A belief that is so very closely tied to your own Self-Worth. As an awakened being, you know that Self is of the utmost importance and is a direct aspect of the Source of All That Is. And so in this respect, you understand that you are a divine expression and that you are here to express and experience individuality, meaning that you are here to express your OWN individual path. Your experiences will not and are not meant to coincide perfectly with any other experiences belonging to another on the planet. The purpose of incarnation is for growth and expansion of THE ALL and your growth and expansion will be unique to your own existence. Remember that you must not judge or rate your own path. You must not judge your own experience, your own existence, based on the existence of another. For what works for them will not necessarily work for you.

We ask that you eliminate the need to operate as this imagined "perfect being" that you believe you are to operate as. We ask that you learn to focus on the Joy, learn to focus on what makes you happy and only what makes you happy. We are in no way advocating that you need to drink alcohol, eat certain foods or perform certain activities – to the contrary. We are not telling you to do or not do anything. We are telling you to do whatever feels right to you and what resonates with your current path. For every aspect of your path is essential to your journey and to your overall growth and expansion. Please understand that if it is your desire to participate in certain experiences, then you are not to listen to another, and you are not to diminish the validity of what brings you Joy. But of course, if you do find that in the process of experiencing what it is that you desire that you do not find Joy and instead you find experiences laced with guilt, addictions or Self-Worth issues, then we encourage you to address the core reason for your desires. The decision to shift your point of attraction and choose new experiences is entirely your decision to make, based on the desired resources for your journey. If you choose to change what is in your reality, it should be via your own knowing and your own personal freedom to do so.

So remember, it is most important that you do away with this limiting belief of Perfectionism, as it is a construct created by societal programing that is never in reality attained by anyone. Perfectionism is in reality impossible to obtain, and it is a fools dream to chase. You will always be evolving, and so it is better to understand that you are continuously developing, continuously growing and continuously expanding. There is no end. We will complete this subject for now, and we will return in our next lesson with a limiting belief that is closely tied to this concept of Perfectionism. We will begin a discussion on the limiting belief: Fear of Failure.

LESSON 12
FEAR OF FAILURE

Today's lesson is a very important message to embrace and understand completely. Today's lesson includes data for one of the most pertinent blocks for Lightworkers. Today, we are going to discuss this concept of a Fear of Failure. To begin, we will Recognize the limiting belief and its pattern throughout your physical existence. We will then Analyze how this pattern is affecting your current experience and lastly proceed to Re-Strategize and begin the process of transmutation.

When we refer to a Fear of Failure, what is that we mean? The Fear of Failure for a Lightworker goes far beyond a simple fear of not completing a task. It goes far beyond the miniscule completion of a task such as getting to the dentist on time or completing a work assignment. No, this Fear of Failure is all encompassing and all devouring, if you do not learn to control it. This fear is in relation to completing this life's Global Purpose. This encompassing fear that you will never be ready to be an example and that you will never be able to overcome your own thoughts, in order to assist the world in overcoming theirs. This devouring thought that you will never be ready, and then you will fail and let everyone down.

For most Lightworkers, this fear of letting everyone down generally doesn't even include the fear of letting themselves down, it is most always the fear of letting others down. When we initially address this, we can see that this fear of letting others down is again a branch off of your own Self-Worth issues. For if you truly cared for Self, you would primarily be concerned about Self. Of course, there is so much more to this concept, but we simply want to draw your attention to how one limiting belief has led into another. As a result, we must eliminate them systematically and as one or they will only continue to exist through each other. Let us delve further into this concept of the Fear of Failure. We will once again begin by addressing your past life experiences and how these energetic imprints in the collective consciousness are affecting your Fear of Failure in this life.

We must stress again that when we address past lives, we only encourage the study of them for the purpose of healing and ultimately allowing Joy in your current experiences. We do not condone delving into past lives as a way to escape current experiences and allow in even more pain. We simply address what must be addressed so you have an understanding of how to overcome in your present experience. In understanding this, let us move forward. When we address this Fear of Failure, it is very important to understand your Global Purpose throughout your ENTIRE collective of incarnations on this planet. You came forward in each life to bring forth knowledge and light into the collective, to keep the Truths tangible in your human histories. You incarnated with purpose each life, and when we say purpose, we mean that each life was lived with the purpose of leading up to this life.

This life, where you would return and put it all together. A time when all of your hard work would pay off, and you would assist others in ascending and, ultimately, ascend your Self.

Let us discuss this concept further. If you are nearing the end of your earthly race and if you have lapped the track so many times so to speak, this would indicate that at the end of your past lives your task and your ultimate goal was not completed. For most of you, the end of these past lives did not end in a blissful encounter filled with roses and sunshine. No, it was essential for the growth of the collective that many of your lives ended gruesomely and tragically. And so for many of you, at the end of these lives you perceived a great sense of failure. Although you have aligned Authentic Self many times in your past lives, and although you understood your ultimate global purpose, you still felt as though you had not completed your task upon departing the physical world. This may be perceived as a hindrance, but please remember that it was this perceived failure that kept you tied to the reincarnation cycle. You had to feel as though you were not finished. You had to desire further growth and expansion. It simply had to be so that you would incarnate with the intention of existing in this life.

When we address this Fear of Failure concept, please remember that this has been a reoccurring theme for you in past lives, so it is no wonder that it would be available to you via the Collective Consciousness, in this life. Let us now move forward into this current aspect of Self. Let us discuss how this Fear of Failure is affecting you now. In your life, due to Self-Worth issues and this overwhelming sense of a need for Perfectionism, a Fear of Failure is very evident for you and the majority of Lightworkers.

You may feel as though you are not good enough for this task, that you are an imposter of some sort and that you will never achieve this perfect image of a spiritual example that you have created in your mind. You think so poorly of your Self and forget that you are a supreme being. You are not your body, not really, you are an infinite creator, and you are an aspect of the Source! Failure is not an option for you! And so we ask that you begin to look at things a little differently. Instead of reliving this old sense of fear, instead of allowing this fear to fester, let us look at it from a different perspective.

When you were younger, let us imagine that you were not raised in the family you were raised in; let us imagine that you were raised somewhere isolated in the mountains. Imagine you were raised by a very spiritual family, one who encouraged your abilities from the beginning. They taught you to channel and taught you to manifest all that you desire. They taught you all of the Laws and Truths that you are learning now. Imagine this life without all of the programming you received in your youth. Imagine where you would be now? Would you have these Self-Worth, Self-Sacrifice and Perfectionism limiting beliefs? Of course not! You would not have the programming that resulted in who you currently are – the current version of Self you are operating as. Now imagine this concept of a Fear of Failure? Would this affect the parallel version of you? Of course not! As a very young child, you would understand your past life fears and possess the knowhow to overcome them. Of course you would not fear failure because your true knowing would have been nurtured within you from the very beginning.

Take a moment to ponder: if your character could change from merely the experiences you acquired and participated in as a child, does this not suggest that the "you" personality is in reality a misconception? Is it not in reality only a product of the environment you found your Self in? And if that product could change depending on the circumstances, can it not be seen that in reality, your physical "you" personality is not you. The True You would not have ceased to exist if you were raised differently; Self would still exist, but only the current version of Self you are operating as would be different based on the data collected. If even one aspect of your childhood changed, and if even the smallest of events occurred, this could have changed your entire perspectives. Now, let us relate this concept back to your current life. Let us acknowledge how "who you are" – physically speaking – is merely the product of programming. With these new understandings, can you not see that this programming is so very easily overcome? All you must do is add new programming and the version of Self will operate so very differently, with such different perspectives.

Now with this valuable perspective, let us once again tackle this concept of a Fear of Failure. Let us address this from an understanding that this Fear of Failure is only stemming from the limiting beliefs of Self-Worth and Perfectionism. Let us acknowledge the part your past lives have played in it all, but remember that this is only a small fraction of the fear. Past life data is only allowed in this life because of your accumulated limiting data. If limiting data were not collected from the experiences you obtained throughout this life – if your past lives were understood and your spiritual nature embraced – past life fears would have no ground to stand on and would be irrelevant data.

However, when past life data is pooled with the various streams of similar data from this life, all contribute to a very powerful limiting belief. And so we say in relation to this concept of a Fear of Failure, you must first come to understand how data is collected and how data contributes to the current version of Self. You must come to understand that this Fear of Failure only exists as a result of the precursor Core Limiting Beliefs that essentially contribute to it. When we say contribute to it, what we mean is that these limiting beliefs merely stack upon each other. There exists base Core Limiting Beliefs that factor into another and another and so forth. We have addressed these limiting beliefs in the order that we have because it is these Core Limiting Beliefs that contribute to and create all other limiting beliefs. By targeting the base of the fears – the Four Core Limiting Beliefs – it will become much easier to eradicate all limiting beliefs quickly and efficiently.

Therefore, we ask that you address this concept of a Fear of Failure knowing that it has stemmed solely from your Self-Worth issues and from your need for Perfectionism. Once you fully allow your Self to embrace and transmute these Self-Worth issues and transmute this fear of Perfectionism, then the process of eliminating the Fear of Failure will be possible. For in reality, when you understand your great importance, when you understand your role, when you understand the magnificence of Self and when you understand the true Spiritual Being that you are, you recognize that Failure is not an option. Failure is of Ego Self, and you are Authentic Self and do not operate as Ego Self. Failure is based on old programming, programming that no longer serves you. Programming that you are eliminating and programming that you are overcoming so that fear no longer holds you.

We are complete on this subject, as we feel that additional understandings and acceptances must be achieved, and so we will begin the next lesson by delving further into the core concepts and the Core Limiting Beliefs that we have discussed thus far.

LESSON 13
THE FOUR CORE LIMITING BELIEFS

We will begin Lesson 13 with a brief recap of what we have addressed thus far. By this point, you have a good understanding of the Core Limiting Beliefs. You recognize that when we say Core Limiting Beliefs, we are proposing that it is these Four Core Limiting Beliefs that are the foundation of all Limiting Beliefs that you will encounter within your life. It is these Four Core Limiting Beliefs that must be addressed in a systematic order to ensure the successful progressive elimination of all the limiting beliefs that no longer serve you. This process need only take as long as you desire it to take. If you are diligent – if you hide nothing from your Self and us – this will be a brief experience, and we will move together onto greater Universal Truths and understandings in no time. Now, you can also choose the alternative approach. You can choose to ignore the feelings and emotions that fester as a result of collected data. You can choose to fight against this process of reprogramming, but as a result you will find this to be a very painful experience. So we ask you now – we plead with you – to set the intention to bring all to the light of truth; set this intention and mean it. We want nothing more than for you to live in Joy and peace at all times. We know that in reaching this desired state of being, you will not only change your life, but you will forever change the collective and create a ripple effect of awakenings – simply through your own acceptance of All That Is. Today, we will begin this lesson with this gentle reminder in the hopes that we will breeze through this process together and in the hopes that you find this remainder of the journey to be pleasant and Joyful.

Today, we would like to further your understandings on the Four Core Limiting Beliefs proposed in the previous chapters. We understand that you may not yet fully grasp the connection between these Core Limiting Beliefs and all perceived negative situations you find your Self in, but we assure you that the connection is very real. We want to impress upon you today that these Core Limiting Beliefs are all that need be addressed to find the balance you seek. Know that it is not necessary to analyze every single offshoot limiting belief, as this process would take FOREVER and would focus your thoughts where they should not be. What we propose is that you fully accept and eliminate the Four Core Limiting Beliefs, and in doing so, all other limiting beliefs will simply fall away. Like a child who has recently learned to walk, you would not resort to crawling again merely because you fall and find your Self back on all fours. No, like this child, you will encounter old resistance with new understandings of how to overcome it. You will approach these offshoot limiting beliefs with new tools and new insights, allowing you to instantly know how to get back up and move forward solidly on your feet. When you encounter these offshoot limiting beliefs, they will provide little resistance because the new data you are collecting now will allow you to logically see in an instant how these limiting beliefs are irrelevant and how newly collected data essentially trumps this old data. You will quickly and efficiently begin to acknowledge that this old data no longer serves you and move freely and easily into a state of Authentic Self Alignment, if you in fact even find that a disconnect has occurred. We call this process "Shifting on Command," and it is a most wonderful tool to learn.

In order to fully grasp and understand this Four Core Limiting Belief concept, it is first important to remember one golden rule. Anytime and we mean EVERY time that you find your Self faced with a limiting belief, this has only occurred as a result of an Authentic Self disconnect. And so in this respect, this means that the heart of any perceived "problem" is the denial of your power. In all cases, the fundamental issue to address is your misguided belief that you are a weak and powerless being, that you are merely meant to flow with the circumstances that you find your Self in and that you have no power or control, at all, over your existence. Believing that you live and die based on chance and that you can only hope that you are not dealt a "crappy" hand is the very heart of all illusion. When you are faced with any limiting belief, before you begin the process of "Recognize, Analyze and Re-Strategize," you must first acknowledge that by choosing to allow this limiting belief you have robbed your Self of your power. You must first affirm that you are a powerful, creative being who is completely and solely responsible for your existence and that this situation you find your Self in is because you have temporarily denied your own power. From this vantage point, you then allow Authentic Self to emerge. You allow Self to realign, and you allow Higher Self to step back into the driver seat so that Authentic Self is operating in perfect alignment. From this mindset, you can clearly and productively address the situation and determine what opportunity has presented itself for growth and expansion. This process will take practice the first few times, but eventually you will – in this moment of remembering your power – become present enough to halt any re-launching of Ego Self.

From this perspective, let us now delve deeper into these Four Core Limiting Beliefs. It should be clear now how these Four Core Beliefs seamlessly flow into one another, and that only through tackling them systematically can you achieve any real results. Now for the sake of programming, it is essential that further understandings are embraced. Not only must we address these limiting beliefs and provide new data to create new patterns and beliefs, but we must also "Re-Strategize" to determine what route you would like to take in your new experiences. As we have said before, this process of analyzing the past is merely to observe the data and determine if this is an experience you would like to repeat or not. From here, we would like to introduce you to another concept that will be discussed in greater detail in an upcoming lesson. This concept of the Two Methods of Creation you can choose from when you encounter any and all beliefs: Maintain or Transmute & Initiate. These are the only choices available to you and these understandings will assist you greatly in the "Re-Strategize" process. So let us briefly explain what we mean by this.

When you are presented with a limiting belief, you must first "Recognize" the Core Limiting Belief and the pattern of this belief throughout your life, via observation of the data collected during experiences. You must then "Analyze" how this Core Limiting Belief and continual pattern is affecting your current experience to determine how you desire to move forward. Following Recognize and Analyze, you will then find your Self at the stage of "Re-Strategize." At this stage, you will use the understandings of Maintain or Transmute & Initiate. You will analyze all data and determine if this limiting belief is something you would like to maintain. At this point in your reading you might say, "Of course I would not want to maintain that which does not serve me!" But for many, they are not truly ready to practice the mental discipline involved in the next steps. If you choose that you truly do not want to maintain this data so that you do not further the limiting belief and pattern in your experiences, you are then left with the option of Transmute & Initiate. Since you have determined that you do not want to maintain the data from the experiences you have observed, you now have the opportunity to Transmute. To fully allow yourself to Transmute your current point of attraction will require mental discipline on your part. By making the choice to Transmute, you are consciously choosing to no longer harbor thoughts related to this limiting belief, and you are choosing to step into your power and embrace the experiences you want to see in your life. From this point of Transmutation, you can then proceed to Initiate the creation of the experience that you wish to see. Now understand, using the processes presented takes great mental discipline and practice, but performing these processes and repeating the steps will allow your mind to refocus on What Is and shift you back to your current intentions.

Let us use a hypothetical example:

Let us say that we are examining a limiting belief related to Self-Worth. Let us say that we are examining past data where you have always felt as though you were an outcast. In your current experience, this limiting belief has surfaced as you find your Self at work during your lunch break feeling alone and as though you are the outcast – yet again. There are others around you, but their actions and their words do not resonate with you, and, yet again, you find your Self submersing back into your own thoughts – wishing you were around others like your Self. So at this point, we can so very easily recognize the limiting belief and pattern. We know that this clearly stems from Self-Worth issues and a feeling that you are so very different – a feeling that you do not fit into society and the Ego Self driven mindsets of many individuals. You can so very easily recognize how this repeated pattern of feeling isolated, as a result of Self-Worth issues, has manifested into your current experience, yet again. You acknowledge these things and decide that you want something different for Self; you decide that you desire a new experience! Now you are presented with an opportunity. Having Recognized the pattern of the Core Limiting Belief and having Analyzed its effect on your current experience, you are now presented with the opportunity to Re-Strategize.

You now know why your Self-Worth is low. You know it is a combination of past lives of feeling like an outcast and current societal programing. You know that in reality you are a very powerful being, and so you know that there is no need for you to feel out of place and strange. You know that you have a divine purpose to fulfill, and you do not need to feel ashamed for being different. From this perspective, you can now choose how you would like to Re-Strategize your future experiences. You have chosen that you no longer wish to maintain this limiting belief and pattern, and so you choose to Transmute this belief and the emotions tied to it. You choose to Initiate a new creation and a new reality for Self. You choose to spend your lunch in happy thoughts. You choose to actively participate in lunch conversations, speaking your own truths and fearlessly directing your own thoughts with compassion and understanding for the current path of others. You no longer choose to sit feeling weird and strange, and instead you choose to attract others that wish to converse about subjects that are uplifting and Joyous. You choose to be the example you are meant to be. Now we do not claim that you would have these interactions with the same coworkers that you would normally converse with, as like can only attract like, but through your example, you would encourage others to want to enrich themselves and their experiences. If you find your Self far too worried that others will judge you for speaking your own Truths when the opportunity presents itself, perhaps this is another opportunity to Recognize, Analyze and Re-Strategize!

We will now conclude this lesson and leave you to ponder these concepts. We will begin the next lesson with a recap of the Four Core Limiting Beliefs, the Three Steps of Realization and the Two Methods of Creation.

LESSON 14
THE THREE STEPS OF REALIZATION

We will begin today with a brief recap of what has been discussed in the previous lessons. From your current perspectives, you understand that there are Four Core Limiting Beliefs that present the foundation for all limiting beliefs. The succession of limiting beliefs will cease to exist when the Four Core Limiting Beliefs are properly understood and their theories denied. You understand that when addressing any limiting belief, you must first Recognize the pattern and the Core Limiting Belief that has created said pattern, Analyze how it is affecting your current experience and then utilize your two choices in the third step of Re-Strategize. You must choose to Maintain your current vibrational alignment or to Transmute it. From this choice of transmutation springs the allowance of a new creation. That is all there is to it. It is not more complicated than this, and yet there is so much more to understand. Today, we would like to delve further into these concepts and develop a routine to assist you in reprogramming limiting beliefs in all aspects of your life.

To begin this discussion, you must first understand that when you encounter ANY limiting belief – and we mean ANY belief that does not serve you – we ask that you do not bother your Self with focusing on the why? When we say "the why," we mean in terms of searching for the physical world understanding of why. For example: let's say you were abused by your father and that these events contributed greatly to many limiting beliefs. You can spend hours and hours pondering, from a physical perspective, what could have led to this experience. You could analyze your father's actions and your actions until you are blue in the face. This will not get you anywhere. What must first be achieved is a recognition of the fact that all experiences have occurred for a reason. You must then acknowledge that your path – precisely the way it was experienced – was essential for your desired growth and expansion, as was your father's. You must acknowledge that all events that took place on his part were but a reflection of his own programming and you CANNOT, no matter how hard you try, truly understand his own perspectives, as these perspectives are unique to his own existence. What you must do in this circumstance is offer compassion and acceptance of the situation. You must understand that all that occurred was necessary for the collective growth and expansion of all parties involved. From this perspective, you are now able to complete the Three Steps of Realization. With this method, you will utilize the past as it was meant to be used and merely compile data to determine what new experiences you would like, based on the data presented.

From this point, you can now begin Step One of the Three Steps of Realization. You can now address the offshoot limiting belief and Recognize the Core Limiting Belief(s) within, as well as the pattern(s) of the core belief(s) that has existed throughout your life. You can now Recognize without limited senses and without limiting interpretations of the situation. You can now understand that all came as a result of the Four Core Limiting Beliefs. From here, you can now move onto Step Two of the Three Steps of Realization. In this step, you will Analyze how the limiting belief you are addressing, and ultimately, the Core Limiting Belief, is affecting your current experience. This process (as well) need not go into extensive analysis. Merely acknowledge how this pattern is reflecting in your current experience and proceed to Step Three of the Three Steps of Realization. Now you are ready to Re-Strategize. When proceeding to Step Three of the Three Steps of Realization, you are presented with a new set of tools that we refer to as the Two Methods of Creation: Maintain or Transmute & Initiate. Based on the data reviewed in the Recognize and Analyze steps, you can now make your choice and determine your next experiences. These two choices are relevant when determining ALL experiences. They are useful when addressing limiting beliefs, but they are also essential when creating in general.

At this stage of pending transmutation, it is so important to remember that limiting beliefs exist for a reason. They exist for your reprogramming journey, and they exist to serve the purpose of creating the beautiful aspect that is Self. So during this process, please do not look at it as though you are doing away with some sort of "BAD" part of you. This is not the case. This is an essential part of you. Merely look at this process as though you are upgrading your knowledge, and as a result, you will achieve a balance and perfect integration between both sets of programming. You will, through this integration, utilize all data seamlessly as Self 2.0. Viewing your limiting beliefs in such a light will assist you in ensuring that you do not unknowingly create further Attachment to that which you are trying to release. Accept them for their role, and allow them to exist peacefully – as a once necessary part of Self.

So let us continue with this most important discussion. When you reach the stage where you are able to utilize the Two Methods of Creation, you are presented with two choices in all of your creations – not only when faced with limiting beliefs. You have the choice to maintain, if the current creation you find your Self in is desired. However, if you do not find that you particularly enjoy the current experience you find your Self in, you are presented with the opportunity of transmutation and ultimately the initiation of a new creation. Now please understand, during this process, it is essential that you release all ties to that which you do not want. Let us explain further.

Let us use an example:

Let us say that you desire more money. Okay, that is just fine. You find your Self in a monetary deficit, yet again, and you wonder where this lack stems from. You ponder what limiting beliefs have led to your current situation. When addressed, you see that this goes right back to the Four Core Limiting Beliefs. You realize that you feel you do not deserve to have financial freedom for some reason – be it as a result of Self-Worth data, Self-Sacrifice data or Perfectionism data. Perhaps you feel you are not worthy of money, and/or that as a spiritual person, you are not to want money, and/or that others do not have money and you feel guilty having it when they do not, etc. There are so many ways this can manifest, but nonetheless, you Recognize where this stems from for you and how it has repeatedly affected your experiences. You then proceed to Analyze how this limiting belief is affecting your current experience. You see that you feel terrible having no money. You see that you are suffering and spending far too much time struggling against this concept of money, instead of truly enjoying your life. You choose to be free of this. From this perspective, you now choose that you are ready to Re-Strategize and utilize the Two Methods of Creation. You determine that you most certainly do not want to maintain your current creation. You determine that you would like to Transmute this vibrational attraction, and so at this point, you choose to no longer focus your thoughts and vibrational frequency on this limiting belief of not deserving and permitting money. You choose to no longer allow any thoughts about the lack that you no longer wish to experience. You decide that you will release all fears associated with money, and in doing so, you will allow financial freedom to flow to you, easily and with little effort on your part.

From this point of transmutation, you then allow Self to STOP attracting an insufficient amount of money and move onto allowing a new creation. Let us stress that you CANNOT attract anything of a new vibration until you STOP attracting that which you are currently attracting. You must release the vibrational attraction from that which you no longer desire, through the transmutation of your thoughts and vibrational frequency. When you achieve this state, you are now ready to Initiate the creation of what it is you desire: be it a set dollar amount, a continuous flow of financial means via your career, or one of your many other options. The choice is yours, but you cannot proceed to initiate a new creation until you have successfully transmuted and released your current point of attraction.

In time, the Three Steps of Realization will be but a brief process in your mind, happening almost simultaneously. With practice, you will instantly Recognize the Core Limiting Belief and pattern, Analyze how it is affecting your current experience and directly proceed to Re-Strategize and utilize the Two Methods of Creation. For many, you will get to a point where you no longer find any time is spent on limiting beliefs, and you are quickly and efficiently able to utilize your understandings to move past any discomfort caused, instantaneously.

That is all for now. In the next lesson we are going to delve deeper into the Two Methods of Creation, allowing you to obtain a proper understanding of how exactly you Transmute what you no longer desire and how you Initiate a new creation.

LESSON 15
TRANSMUTE & INITIATE

We will begin this lesson with a brief recap of what we have learned together. At this point, you fully understand the Four Core Limiting Beliefs. You understand that they are the foundation for all limiting beliefs, and by addressing the root of these beliefs, you will then be able to systematically transmute any and all offshoot limiting beliefs. You understand the Three Steps of Realization process, and you understand the importance of: Recognize and Analyze. You have begun to implement these steps in your daily life, and you are learning to shift on command. Today, we are going to delve deeper into Re-Strategize, the last step of the Three Steps of Realization. We are going to begin one of many lessons on the Transmute & Initiate choice of the Two Methods of Creation.

Firstly, it is important to understand that when we address the Two Methods of Creation in the context of overcoming limiting beliefs, our goal is never choice one. We are never intending to maintain a limiting belief. For the purpose of the lessons in this chapter, we will focus primarily on choice two and address choice one, the concept of Maintain, in an upcoming chapter when we teach you to create the reality you desire. So for now, when we address the Two Methods of Creation, we will refer only to choice two: Transmute & Initiate.

So what exactly is this process of transmutation that we have referred to on numerous occasions? The process of transmutation, simply put, is to change form. In this case, what we are attempting to transmute is the vibrational frequency currently being offered that is resulting in the "unwanted" manifested physical situations you find your Self in. Now let us delve deeper. From what you have learned so far, you understand that all thoughts create a vibrational frequency that mirrors onto the physical plane. You understand that your thoughts have the power to create reality, but we have only begun to scratch the surface of this concept. We have only begun to explain how vibrations create your reality, but we will leave the "in depth" discussions on this concept until Chapter 3 and only discuss the basics now. When we refer to vibrations and their ability to create your reality, we find that many people perceive this concept incorrectly. Many of you find your Selves believing that your negative thoughts are creating that which you do not want. That it is, literally, the negative thought that calls the Law of Attraction into action, which then creates that which you do not want in the physical. In actuality, this is not entirely accurate.

To understand the concept of transmutation, you must first understand what it is that you are changing. Every physical being is connected to higher levels of consciousness through Self. There is never a time that you are disconnected from this extension of Source Energy, as it is this energy that creates your awareness. If a disconnect in fact did occur, this would result in what you perceive as "death." Know that at all times, regardless of whether or not you are being driven by Higher Self or Ego Self, you are always connected to Higher Self and ultimately All That Is.

This connection is your direct link to the Source and your direct link to well-being. Naturally, you are designed to exist in Authentic Self Alignment at all times and to live a life of perfect well-being provided to you in the physical by Higher Self. This direct flow of abundance comes naturally and easily via a beautiful extension of Source Energy: the vibrational frequency that creates All That Is and all that exists in your physical reality. What occurs as a result of programming is that this connect becomes distorted. When discussing this a "stream of water" analogy conveys our understandings quite nicely. When you direct a projectile of water at another, say through a water hose, this projectile will shoot straight at the target. Now suppose that a hand is placed in front of this stream of water, blocking a portion of the water stream. In this case, a portion of the water will still hit the target, but the remaining portion will be disrupted by the blockage and fall to the floor creating a puddle. This is precisely what happens in the creation process for most people. Because you are naturally meant to receive a continuous stream of well-being and an optimal vibrational flow from Source Energy, as we are creators who are meant to live Joyously, there is always a steady flow coming your way. What happens is that your thoughts then offer resistance to this well-being and only allow a fraction of well-being to flow into your experience, thus creating what appears to be a mess from the remaining flow that did not reach its target as intended. This mess is often referred to as miscreation or misdirected Source Energy.

It is in these times of "misdirected" Source Energy where you experience struggle, tragedy, poverty, etc. The degree to which you offer resistance to the direct optimal flow of Source Energy determines the degree to which you experience the above stated undesirable experiences. Now understand this resistance is only offered due to programming, and through reprogramming, you can so very easily learn to stop offering resistance and allow the full flow of well-being into your experience.

Let us return now to this understanding of vibrations. As we have stated above, the water is merely a representation of the optimal vibrational frequency of Source Energy that is naturally flowing to the physical aspect of Self, through the mental plane to then manifest onto the physical plane. Your thoughts determine how this vibrational frequency will manifest. If you offer no resistance via your thoughts, the creation will manifest onto the physical plane as the most ideal creation you could imagine at the time. If you offer resistance, as a result of your programming, your thoughts will take the original optimal vibration, emanating from the spiritual plane, and it will distort it on the mental plane. Your negative thoughts of fear based vibrations will essentially, via the law of attraction, only allow that original optimal vibration to manifest on the physical plane in accordance with your vibrational frequency offered on the mental plane. So let us look at this way: your mind simply acts as a filter. Your mind has the ability to allow every bit of well-being to flow and pass through unaltered, or your mind has the ability to filter the optimal vibration in accordance with the limiting beliefs you allow to create said filter. There is never a case where this optimal vibrational frequency can pass without your allowance of it. It is the law of physical existence.

This is the choice that was made to provide Self with free will. If you choose to harbor thoughts of low Self-Worth and Self-Sacrifice, then you will not allow the optimal vibrational frequency to pass, and you will essentially allow your limiting beliefs to filter and determine what the best is for you at the time. Now that being said, you can just as easily determine that you will no longer stand for the filtering of your creations, as a result of limiting programming, and you can choose to remove this filter and all limiting beliefs, thus allowing your Self to create your Heaven on Earth. The choice is yours. It is no more difficult to allow one over the other, unless you believe it to be so. As a Conscious Creator, you can create anything you desire, and it is only your limiting beliefs that have made you forget this fact.

Let us recap what we have learned. You have a continuous flow of well-being directing at you at all times. Your limiting beliefs offer resistance to this flow and essentially distort the vibrational frequency of your well-being, thus, determining what you allow to manifest on the physical plane. Now, let us return to this concept of transmutation. When we say that you must change the form of the frequency, what we mean is that you must transmute the resistance you are offering, and you must return the vibrational frequency to optimal well-being. This may sound simple, but this is of course something that does require mental focus on your part. A process that need only be as difficult or as easy as you allow it to be. In order for you to create all that you desire on the physical plane, such as more money, health, a loving partner, children, etc., you must learn to transmute all the limiting vibrational frequencies you are offering in respect to these manifestations.

You MUST Recognize & Analyze so that you can determine how you have affected the optimal vibrational frequency of your natural well-being, and in doing so, you can then determine how you would like to proceed moving forward. You can then advance to the Re-Strategize step and instantly transmute the vibration, by acknowledging new data that essential trumps old understandings. It is in this moment, when you acknowledge that you have distorted your natural optimal vibrational frequency that you allow a transmutation to begin and open the doors to a new Joyous creation.

Once you have determined that you would like to see a new experience in your reality, you then begin the process of Initiate. It is during this step that you have your fun. It is during this step that you dream big and allow the optimal vibration, so that you begin shifting your attraction on the physical plane. It is during this step that you not only transmute what you have currently been attracting, you also proceed to initiate a new creation all together. We will end our communication on these understandings for now and pick up in the next lesson, delving further into this process of Transmute & Initiate.

LESSON 16
TRANSMUTE & INITIATE - PART II

There is much to discuss in this lesson so that we may proceed to Chapter 3 and commence with Reality Creation. We will begin with a brief recap of what we have learned thus far. By now you should fully comprehend the Four Core Limiting Beliefs. You should understand the Three Steps of Realization and how to properly utilize them to shift back into Authentic Self Alignment. As well, you should have a basic understanding of the process involved in the Two Methods of Creation. Today, we would like to further your understandings on the Two Methods of Creation and provide a precursor into the upcoming chapter.

What we have learned thus far suggests strategies that offer you the opportunity to leave behind that which no longer serves you. We have suggested strategies so that you could allow your Self to choose what you are to focus on and ultimately create in your reality. We have done so for two very important reasons. Firstly, it is only through a healed vessel that you can truly assist the world, and secondly, we are preparing you for what will be taught in the upcoming chapter: Creating Your Heaven on Earth. Our primary focus with this channel is, and will always be, awakening Lightworkers so that they may begin creating their own individual utopias. In doing so, we will create a light so great in the Collective Consciousness that the world will begin to resemble this drastic shift of forward thinking. These Lightworkers, YOU to be more accurate, exist in this time for a very important reason: for growth and expansion, of course, but as we have said before – this lifetime is very different. Your primary focus in this life is to use the tools and knowledge that you have gained throughout your succession of lives as a human and/or other worldly being. You will use this knowledge, putting to test all that you have acquired throughout your eons of existence and YOU WILL change the world.

How will you do this you might ask? It is simple. You will do it through Joy; you will do it through laughter; you will do it through living a life so marvelous and beautiful that others will be in awe and want what you have. You will do it through changing archaic beliefs and by blowing the notion that as humans you are merely prey to circumstances, right out of the water. How will you do it? By creating your Heaven on Earth.

On a superficial level, it will appear to others that you have created a world so marvelous that it defies physical world logic, but much deeper, you will know the truth. You will have simply reprogrammed your mind and, in doing so, harnessed the true power of Self. As a result, you will have defied what others said was impossible, and you will have proven that YOU choose your reality. Not only will you again, as you have done in previous lives, create tangible Truths of that which you know to be true, you will also create a crack in the solidified archaic views of the Collective Mind, and you will shatter all preconceived notions of who you truly are! You will change the world, BUT this can only begin with your reprogramming.

Now that we have shown where we shall proceed, let us continue with our discussion on what must first be understood and acknowledged. You want the scenario discussed above, do you not? You want your Heaven on Earth, you want your piece of paradise? Of course, you do. It is only natural as a Lightworker to know that you deserve to have all that you desire. Deep down you have always had dreams of what you wanted out of this life. Dreams that you shut out because of the numerous limiting beliefs you have acquired over time. You have always wanted these things, but you have allowed the limitations and opinions of others to break you of your hopes and dreams. Today, we do away with this. Today, we say: no more. Today, we ask you to remember who you are and what you are capable of. Today, we ask you to remember that you are a Divine Creator, and anything and everything that you desire is yours. You will achieve this glorious state of paradise, and ultimately Heaven on Earth, but first you must let go of what you no longer wish to experience.

Sounds so simple, yes? So easy to just say, "Okay, I let it go!" and then allow the new experiences you desire in. It is so simple, and yet it can often be so difficult for the human mind to comprehend. As we have been where you are, we do understand just how difficult this can appear to be, but we assure you as we have always said, this need only be as difficult as YOU make it. In reality, this is an easy process for you. In actuality, you need only gain the data required to run the Self program that will allow you to fully acknowledge your power. In reality, this could be achieved instantaneously, but of course, you would offer resistance to such a quick and brash download of information; so we will make this process slower and teach you what you must first be taught. During this process, we ask you to be patient and know that you will achieve what you desire – it is a guarantee – but you must first take the necessary steps to get there. You want this process to go quickly? This is most excellent, and if you do – then let it go! Let go of your Attachment to what you have now, and you will achieve the transmutation required to initiate the receiving of your new desired creations in the physical world! When you ask of and ponder this concept of Transmutation, it really is that simple.

To truly allow your Self to let go, you must learn to see past the illusion of Duality and view all creations in your life as neither good nor bad. Now please understand, we do not say this so that you deny what is occurring in your life. We say this so that you can stop with the Attachments to what you say you do not want in your life. We are not asking you to pretend that something undesirable is not happening to you; we simply want you to acknowledge the Neutrality of it all. You may be sick, you may be broke, you may be alone and without a partner? Okay, so what? This is neither good nor bad; this is merely a point of attraction. This is merely the current state that you have attracted. You are a Divine Creator; therefore, as you have created the physical reality you see before you, you can so very easily create a new desired physical reality. It is no more difficult than that, but first you must do away with your Attachments to your creations. You must stop viewing the world as this dualistic place of "good" situations in opposition with "bad" situations and of "wanted" creations struggling against "unwanted" creations. Believe us, there are no unwanted creations and there are no bad creations. There is simply What Is. In the same respect, there are no situations that are superior or better either – dualistically speaking. All simply IS and is merely a point of attraction. What you deem to be good or bad is merely a reflection of your own personal perspectives, and this judgment will differ from person to person as an echo of your unique individual personalities. There is no good vs. bad; there is no light vs. dark. There is only What Is and there is only choice!

Now let us explain this further. To deem something as better or to deem something as superior is not in itself what limits you – it is the logic and belief surrounding this dualistic desire. If your intention is clear and you desire something purely to experience a new situation, knowing that it is your natural birth right to be able to do so, then your intention is pure and of a non-dualistic nature. Now on the other hand, if you are perceiving an experience as "superior" or "better" to another in the sense of Duality, this is what you are really saying: you are saying that one experience/creation is required simply because the opposite of this experience/creation, being the bad and unwanted, is not desired. You are using what is "better" and "superior" as a means to try to escape from that which you perceive as the unwanted alternative. Thus, creating an Attachment to both the perceived "good" and the perceived "bad," due to the limiting fear surrounding the desire. And from this perspective, your attention is focused on the perceived positive of an experience/creation only out of fear of the negative dual opposite.

When you perceive the world in a dualistic nature, you do not understand or appreciate that all of your perceived "negative," "unwanted" or "bad situations" are in fact wonderful and important tools to redirect you and help you determine what it is you truly desire. You do not see that these experiences are essential to determining what limiting beliefs must be transmuted so that you may move forward in your growth and expansion. When you view experiences and creations as "bad" or "unwanted," you in essence run and hide from them in fear instead of learning from them. You do not realize that your fears keep you tied to what you say you do not want. You will not move forward until you understand that in reality there is nothing to be conquered. There is only what IS, which is attempting to teach you for your desired growth. There is only what has been attracted, and it is neither good nor bad. To judge is to condemn your Self into a continual pattern of what you say you do not want. See past the illusion of the struggle of Duality and see that all is wanted, all is necessary and ALL is assisting you on your path. There is, in reality, no Light nor Dark, no Good nor Bad, no continual struggle between opposites. There is only ONE and there is only What IS. ALL is of the same Source.

As a result of this judgment thinking, you tend to bury data deep down; you tend to sweep it under the rug and simply say, "This is unwanted, and I know what I want and I will only focus on that because I most certainly do not want the "bad" alternative." You ignore the blatant fears that are the cause of your obsessive need to fixate on the "good," which you believe will free you of the unwanted and the "bad." You fail to see that all manifestations that appear in the physical are simply by-products of the programming that exists in your mind: programming that is only manifesting to show you where reprogramming is needed. This programming cannot simply be ignored but must instead be balanced out to allow the transmutation you desire. You must remove the fear and embrace What Is and what has been called forward to assist you! If you proceed to use the fearful unnecessary "sweep under the rug" strategy, you will only discover that your thoughts do not change and that the same data still finds a way to continuously manifest into your life time and time again.

However, if you are to do away with a dualistic nature and determine that there are no unwanted experiences – no good or bad creations – you will come to realize that there are merely experiences, or points of attraction, which provide wonderful tools and insights into your thoughts. Having this most important information is essential in allowing you to see where reprogramming is needed. So remember, there are no good or bad creations; there is simply What Is and what you have attracted based on your current programming and the current version of Self you are operating as. When you understand and accept this, you will reach a most marvelous state of consciousness where you are ready to create your Heaven on Earth. From this understanding of non-duality, you will view all experiences as precious and all experiences as wanted and desired. You will view your life from a new perspective and acquire new understandings for "dualistic" words and terms. Words such as wanted, good, and Joy will no longer represent an option of Duality. The words will no longer have a darker side. There is only light, there is only good, there is only wanted, and there is only Joy. This is the

Truth if you allow it to be so. From this perspective and state of consciousness, you will begin to immediately notice when you have viewed an experience from a dualistic mindset and shifted from Authentic Self Alignment. You will recognize a situation that is attempting to teach you something, via your Emotional Indicator, and you will be most pleased with this opportunity to Recognize, Analyze and Re-Strategize so that you may Transmute the limiting belief that no longer serves you, and as a result, find your Self one step closer to your Heaven on Earth.

So when you wonder what it truly means to transmute, know this: transmutation is simply letting it go. Transmutation is allowing in the necessary data to see that there is no duality – no good or bad, no wanted or unwanted and no right or wrong. There are NO opposites in opposition; no struggle between What IS. There are simply points of attraction. All situations are beneficial, and your Emotional Indicator is a marvelous tool to show you where new data is required and where transmutation is needed. All that exists in your experience is marvelous and wonderful and IS the universe attempting to assist you in your goal of creating your Heaven on Earth. After all, that is a primary part of your Global Purpose. You are here to show others the light of Truth. You are here to heal the true insanity in the world. You are here to show those around you that there is another way; a way of Joy, peace and abundance. But you can only show this by being an example of it. Do your part and work diligently. Do not give up and have faith, because you child will succeed, and you will change this world forever.

~We want you to remember the primary reason for your existence. You are here to create your Heaven on Earth. You are here to set an example for all those incarnated so that you may represent the true scope of your potential and the potential of others. You are to set an example and show the world precisely who you truly are. This cannot be achieved by pretending that you are whole and healed, and this can most certainly not be achieved by showing others a light that you, your Self, have not fully embraced.~

CHAPTER 3

CREATING YOUR HEAVEN ON EARTH

CHAPTER 3
INTRODUCTION

We are so pleased to have reached this point of our journey together. There is still much to be done in regards to reprogramming, but this will all occur in time and in accordance with your individual path. All the data that you are receiving now will essentially accelerate your own path of ascension, and in time, you will find that you have become an expert in all that we have discussed. You will be empowered with truths so great that you will assist in changing the way humanity is understood. You will no longer sit by and allow circumstances to rule you; you will create your circumstances – becoming a master of them – and you will show the world precisely who you truly are.

This chapter will assist you in remembering your natural creative abilities. It will provide you with the means to take what you have learned in the previous chapters and utilize it optimally to allow your Heaven on Earth to materialize around you. You understand who you are now. Moving forward, you understand how to balance all programming that no longer serves you. You are now armed with the ability to control your thoughts enough to start producing tangible evidence reflecting your dedication. As your mind becomes uncluttered, and as you begin to release resistance, you will notice the world around you changes as do your thoughts. You will notice a shift so drastic that you will have undeniable evidence of your power as a Conscious Creator.

As we move onto this next chapter together, be prepared to do your mental homework. Be prepared to leave behind all that no longer serves you. Be sure to choose a mindset of peace and Joy and focus only on that which brings you Joy. We will remain with you through this process, as we always have, and we will work as your co-creators bringing to you that which you desire that much quicker. We are most pleased to be on this journey with you, and we thank you for your dedication thus far. Through receiving this data, you have already created a mighty rift in the Collective Mind that the world around you is manifesting in accordance with the universal laws. We are very proud of you and eager for the journey to come. Love and light, dearest one.

LESSON 17
REALITY CREATION

Chapter three encompasses a subject that fascinates many of you. This concept that you could create your own reality seams so appealing, as deep down you feel the resonance within your natural abundant state of being. You examine this subject knowing your own ability to create, and yet you have programming within you that suggests this simply can't be. You have received data that has led you to believe that you are weak and you are simply a by-product of your circumstances; circumstances that you have no control over. Today, we are going to begin the process of showing you just how inaccurate this notion is.

There is so much to be taught and so much to be learned in regards to this subject, and so, as always, we must start at the beginning. We must start with the basic knowledge so that you may establish the foundational beliefs required to fully understand and embrace your ability to create your own reality. So what can be said about Reality Creation? Firstly, this is something that you are already doing. So many of you look at this concept of Reality Creation and think that it merely applies to "deliberate" conscious reality creation, as has been taught by many people, but that is not what we are referring to here. We are referring to reality creation in general, and the fact is that you are ALWAYS, in every moment of every day, creating your reality. Everything you see before you is a product of your thoughts produced by the current version of Self and is ultimately based on Self's allowing of the best possible well-being. Everything you see around you exists because you have given your attention to it. Now understand in saying this, it should become very obvious that YES – you HAVE chosen everything you see around you.

This is always a hard concept for humans to understand, that you would create the so called "unwanted" situations you find your Self in, but this is the truth nonetheless. Every situation you find your Self in is created by your attraction of it. There are no exclusions to this rule. Many question why one would attract a situation that causes harm or why one so young would attract a situation when they do not consciously understand what has occurred to them. To this we say: you are looking at it inaccurately. There is nothing in your life that is being attracted by your physical body. Now let us explain. The form you see, the body that is reading these words, is not you. This is the Physical Form, the vessel for "you" to experience physicality. The mind that thinks your thoughts, this again is not you. This is simply the operating system of Self – the unbiased regulator of the data so to speak. You are not your Body or your Mind, you are something much greater. You are Higher Self experiencing through the individualized aspect known as "you" – through Self as an integration of Body, Mind and Soul. You are always tethered as your Body, Mind and Soul at all times, even through moments of Ego Self-control

– because remember Ego Self was your creation after all.

All creations that come into your experiences do so from the free will of the True You – Higher Self. All perceived "Bad," "Good" and in-between manifestations come not from your body or mind, but from the true programmer. So from this perspective, let us consider the previous proposed questions. Why would one attract harm and why would one so young attract a situation that they do not understand? Well, for growth and expansion. Again, this is an extremely difficult concept for humans to grasp. You cannot fathom why any being would choose harm for themselves, but understand, all who incarnate have their role to play. In all cases, the decisions of Higher Self are to serve their life's purpose and ultimately the greater purpose of The ALL. In experiencing these things, one can operate as a catalyst for change and/or be presented with a situation that ultimately propels one's Self onto the required path. Many of those who have gone to do great things in the world have done so out of "perceived" terrible situations. It was these situations that caused them to rise up and demand something better for themselves and the world. This is not meant to imply that you should not look at these situations with compassion – understanding that you most certainly would not want anyone to suffer – but you must look at these situations with a non-dualistic mind. You must accept that they are neither good nor bad, but simply points of attraction, necessary for growth and expansion on a personal and global level. In reality, all decisions made by Higher Self that appear to be for personal growth are really for the growth of all, as all is ONE.

So why are we discussing this? Why do we say these things? Simply because you must begin this chapter by accepting accountability. Everything in your life is your doing – not someone else's. Everything, you have allowed. It does not matter what you have been through as a child, the fact is that at some point you – as an awakened being – should be taking control of the situation and you should be accepting accountability. It does not matter what someone did to you in the past, as the past was your choice for growth and expansion. And furthermore, it IS the present now, and it is YOU doing it to you now. You should not stand for this, as it is a blatant denial of your power. It is essential, moving forward in this chapter, that you no longer play the "blame game," and you learn to acknowledge all that has occurred as part of your path; is has been neither good nor bad, but simply points of attraction necessary for growth and expansion.

So moving forward, now that what needs to be addressed has been addressed, let us move onto your next essential understandings. Many of you are still looking at your past as being filled with good or bad experiences. Remember, as we have said, there are no good or bad experiences. There are only points of attraction and choices made for growth and expansion. Many of you have thoughts that come from previous data and you automatically get frustrated, upset or angry, thinking "Why can't I control my thoughts? What am I doing wrong?" Firstly, we must say that you are doing nothing wrong. Remember, this is an essential part of your path and simply an indication that more data is needed for clarity. Secondly, not all thoughts are "thoughts" as you currently understand them. Let us explain further.

Any "thought" that enters the mind is either from past programming or new programming coming in through Authentic Self Alignment, via Higher Self. There are of course opportunities for communication such as these writings, but in these cases, these thoughts are not your own. So let us continue. When you have what you perceive to be a thought, it is either the product of "past" or "present" data. If it is a thought from a past experience, it is essential that you come to understand that these thoughts are not bad! They are merely data attempting to assist you! These thoughts present the opportunity to examine how you have fared in previous similar situations.

For example: When you experience anything in your physical world, your mind will instantly trigger relevant thoughts to what you are observing, to assist you in dealing with your current experience. Regardless if what you are experiencing is perceived as negative or positive, your mind will instantaneously conjure up similar experiences in an attempt to help you make an informed decision. Data can be compiled from a variety of experiences, collected by any of your senses, and essentially, all data within the mind that is similar is considered relevant to bring forward. For example: let us consider when you smell an aroma and your mind takes you back to a childhood memory. This memory is conjured, not because the aroma reminds you of this memory, but because this previous memory is comparable and relevant to the aroma you are experiencing now. The fact is the mind is designed to give you similar data to assist you in moving forward – even in situations involving fear. When you are faced with something you do not like and the mind conjures similar fear based data, it is not doing so to harm you. It is doing so to remind you of what path you took in similar situations. Firstly, so that you can make an informed decision, and secondly, so that you can choose an alternate path if you did not enjoy the previous outcome.

There is no need to yell "NO" to these thoughts, as they are not creating anything; they are merely giving you relevant data. What tends to happen for those of you that do not have the necessary programming is that you choose to fester the thought, which was only meant to be relevant programming. You are not acknowledging that it is your most marvelous mind doing its job and simply giving you data to assist you moving forward. Instead, you essentially send your Self into a panicked state thinking that this relevant data is now somehow predicting you future. You fail to see that this data is only displaying relevant past experiences to assist you in creating a new experience of your choosing. Your mind is only ever trying to assist Self, but you have forgotten the value of this most important tool, and you have forgotten how to respect the power of Self. Instead of having these thoughts and then choosing to create the unwanted by then giving ALL of your attention to this unwanted thing, you should address the thought for what it is: just previously collected data. Simply say, "Thank you mind for this data. Thank you for providing this wonderful previously collected data, which has now shown me that I have experienced ample situations where I did not enjoy the experience of having this in my life. Thank you beautiful mind for telling me so. I now fully recognize that I want a different outcome." From this perspective, you can then choose to shift your attention to choose the outcome you desire! Most of you have forgotten about the function of the mind, and as a result, you have these "data" thoughts and then proceed into a spiral of "unwanted" thoughts, which then proceed to create what you say you do not want. Can you see how unnecessary this all is? All you must do is recognize the data thought for what it is.

Now in terms of present thoughts – let us first address reprogramming, empowering, positive and Joy-based thoughts. Where do you think these thoughts come from? From Higher Self of course – the True You. These thoughts are programming for Self-Realization and result in moments of true knowing and resonance. These thoughts are preparing you for upcoming creations, by giving you wonderful amazing insights into what you would now like to experience. These thoughts are the ones that cause you to create new desires and then give your attention to said desires and direct your reality. These thoughts are essential to deliberately creating. Likewise, as you are able to have present thoughts given by the sole direction of Higher Self, you are also capable of choosing present thoughts that are the product of a more fear based director. The choice is yours. But remember, all is truly stemming from Higher Self, and if you are to re-launch the Ego Self and choose a fear based director, it is simply because there is something to be gained and learned from said experience. ALL that occurs in your physical reality is for the required growth and expansion to achieve what is desired on one's path. All is truly overseen and programmed by Higher Self – for the mere Joy, beauty and challenge of experiencing physical existence through SELF.

In ending this lesson, let us briefly return to this understanding of deliberate creation. Deliberate Reality Creation is simply this: knowing your power to create, knowing that you are always creating and using your amazing mind properly

– to intentionally choose the physical reality you desire to experience next. This is what we will learn in this chapter. You will learn to control your thoughts and not have your thoughts control you! You will learn how to use the knowledge in the previous chapter in correlation with new Truths and you will marvelously create your Heaven on Earth! Very good, friend. We look forward to the next lesson!

LESSON 18
FINDING THE BALANCE

We are most pleased with your progress thus far and are so very excited that you have reached this point in the lessons. We simply cannot contain our overwhelming sense of pride! Although this re-awakening is yours, this is an equally Joyous experience for us as we simply delight in the idea of watching you awaken to your natural abilities! For you see, through you and your Self Expansion, we are experiencing the physical. We are remembering what it is like, and we are gaining a new level of growth and expansion as we serve this great function of assisting from the nonphysical. While you grow and expand through your experiences – so do we! And we love nothing more than to grow and expand! So know this: while we assist you, you are assisting us – greatly – as it is through YOU that we are given the opportunity to participate in physical existence! For that we applaud you and sincerely THANK YOU!

And so let us continue with a brief review of what we have learned. At this point, you have begun to comprehend your part in your reality. You should understand that you are responsible for all that occurs in your experiences. Regardless of programming received throughout your life, you are now going to take accountability and bring all that no longer serves you to the surface for transmutation. We encourage you to continue to practice what has been taught in previous lessons; even though you have now begun the alluring and exciting chapter of Reality Creation. Remain diligent with the transmutation of limiting beliefs that no longer serve you, or you will simply allow old programming to creep in through the back door.

There are many concepts that must be understood and embraced whole heartedly before you can truly let go of all fear and become a successful Conscious Creator. For many of you, you struggle so greatly with letting go of the illusions of the physical world. So much so, that your programming will make any new data/ understandings received a struggle for your mind to comprehend. You may find that this causes an uncomfortable distortion of your reality. Remember, as we have always said, this need only be as difficult or as easy as you allow it to be. If you find your Self faced with resistance and struggle during this process, this is but an indication that you require further clarification. Do not give up and do not give in to old limiting programming. Relax, take a break and realign Self through the knowledge you have been given. Recognize, Analyze and Re-Strategize! Allow your Self to reconnect Authentic Self Alignment, and simply ask, "What am I missing here? What data do I need moving forward to allow a balance in the programming?"

This is precisely what we would like to discuss in this lesson. Today, we want to further your understandings of this concept of "creating a balance" in the programming. As we have always said, there are no bad thoughts and there is no bad programming. All programming is an essential part of you and was essential to get you precisely where you are now. We assure you, without the exact experiences you endured throughout your life, you would not be where you are today. So with this in mind, let us move forward. We understand that many of you struggle greatly with not viewing "Ego Self" programming as bad. As this data was collected when you were not in Authentic Self Alignment, you cannot help but determine that this programming is in itself bad or unwanted. We want to give you an opportunity to truly release this because we assure you, if you continue to view the world in a dualistic manner – if you continue to see the good and the bad – you will find little success as a Conscious Creator.

To consciously create the reality of your choosing, you must learn to give up Attachment in all facets. This means no good or bad, no wanted or wanted. Only choice and only Neutrality. All is beneficial and all is for experience and growth. You must begin to truly grasp this sense of Neutrality, or you will find that you will not allow your Self to fully transmute that which you no longer wish to experience. So where do we go from here? You understand that you must achieve a balance in your programming. It is always about balance, never about deleting or removing anything; all is essential and all is necessary. So from this perspective, we will now offer a strategy so that you may obtain a proper balance in all of your programming. If you do not resonate with the specific strategies or methods that we offer, this is of no concern – simply listen to your own knowing and form your own method. What is most important is that you take the knowledge that we have given and utilize it in some degree. For if you continue on the path of ignorance, and struggle against utilizing the knowledge you have been given, you will find great discomfort and only continue to limit your power. So in saying this, we strongly encourage that you approach all provided knowledge with the utmost of seriousness, because what we offer you is life altering Truths. Remember, we have been where you are many times. We understand this struggle to be human, and so we understand how essential assistance such as this can be. Be diligent and practice, practice, practice. Do not do it simply because we have told you to. Do it because you deserve absolute power, because you deserve optimal experiences, and because you deserve nothing less than pure bliss.

As we have discussed in previous lessons, it is an imbalance of data that results in all reoccurring limiting beliefs and, as a result, continued creation of that which you say you no longer wish to experience. Understand in us stressing the importance of balance, we do it so that you can begin to shift your thoughts and begin the very rewarding process of creating the reality you choose and deserve. All limiting beliefs can be traced back to the Four Core Limiting Beliefs, and utilizing the Three Steps of Realization will be a most rewarding strategy. However, you may find that you have certain beliefs that are in between the phase of Realization through thought and Realization on the physical plane – even though you have practiced the Three Steps of Realization many times. Let us explain further. When you reach this point previously discussed, you will have fully acknowledged a limiting belief, its origins and how it is affecting your current experience. You will then have proceeded to attempt to transmute this belief that no longer serves you but are finding it a struggle to release. It is in this stage that we would like to assist you. At this stage, you acknowledge what is desired moving forward, and you simply need a strategy to quickly and efficiently Transmute this limiting belief by removing your attention to it. In doing so, you will then release your Self of the last remnants of dominant data so that you may be free of it once and for all. Hence, initiating wonderful new creations on the physical plane. All that is required is dedication and the willingness to choose the path of least resistance.

Today, we would like to offer a visualization to assist. We are advocates of visualizations used in a manner that is empowering, not in a manner meant to brainwash. Many people use visualizations more so out of fear, repetitively forcing themselves into this practice merely out of a fear of not achieving the desired results. Remember, ANYTHING that is tainted with the limiting energies of boredom, irritation or a sense of insecurity will not yield beneficial results. When we encourage visualizations, we do so only when they are used in an uplifting manner and only when they are Joyous. If this suggested visualization does not work for you, again, we encourage you to follow your own guidance and find what benefits you.

In this moment when a limiting belief has presented itself, and you are not able to allow it to pass instantaneously because you simply require a little more data to complete the Transmute & Initiate Step, this is what we propose:

We encourage you to view a scale in your mind's eye; a scale similar to those seen in your photos depicting images of justice with two hanging receptacles on either side.

When looking at this scale, you will see that the left side is lower to the ground and filled with more items – depicted how you choose – resulting in the scale being unbalanced. These items represent the data collected in relation to this limiting belief you desire to transmute. What we encourage you to do is place items – depicted how you choose – on the right side of the scale as you recite Joy-based data, in relation to your limiting belief. Then, watch as the scale begins to balance out. This visualization is being presented to allow multiple things to occur: Firstly, it gives an understanding that the past programming that no longer serves you is not to be deleted but merely balanced out with new data of a higher level of consciousness. Secondly, this visualization allows a "distraction" from thoughts directed toward feeding the limiting belief. Lastly, this visualization will allow for the creation of thoughts in favor of that which you desire to see in your experience.

Let us use an example. Let us say that you are having thoughts about money, and a limiting belief in regards to not having enough money has crept into your mind. Because you are having a very active day, you are not able to guard your thoughts as closely as normal. This is of no concern. Immediately, as you have addressed this belief before, you know that this goes back to Self-Worth issues and your denial of your ability to create your own reality as a powerful Conscious Creator. You know that this also stems from feelings of Self-Sacrifice. You recognize that you often feel that you do not deserve to have complete financial freedom –even though to have money and to not have money require precisely the same effort in thoughts and both present neutral creations. You do not need to Recognize, as you have already completed this process. You instantaneously know how this belief has patterned throughout your life and you fully acknowledge how it is affecting your current experience. You are so very close to transmuting this limiting belief once and for all, you are simply working through the last bits of straggling data that you still attached to. So in this moment, you are going to work on the above suggested strategy for instant transmutation. You will shift from offering a vibration of lack and low income to offering a vibration of power, abundance and financial freedom. The moment this familiar limiting belief enters the mind, imagine your scale and begin straight away with placing items on your side of the scale, as you recite Authentic Self data such as this:

"I am a Conscious Creator of my reality. I am a powerful being, and I can create any reality I choose. I now choose to experience complete financial freedom. I choose to have wealth, abundance and a continual flow of the means of exchange for all of the material items I desire to have! I choose to continually attract money, and I allow it to flow freely and easily into my experience. I choose to have financial freedom NOW!"

As you say these things and place items on the right side of the scale as you do so, you will notice the scale begin to balance out. Recite as much Authentic Self data as necessary until the scale balances, you feel empowered and your vibration has shifted to that which you desire to create! Do not be afraid to pile on as many "items" as you desire until you reach the optimal state of Joy. Pile on so many that the scale tips strongly in your favor if you desire, but in reality, the scale will remain in a balanced state. We encourage you to remember that all programming will subside regardless of its reoccurrence in your thoughts. We assure you that this is how it works with the mind; you fester, fester, fester, but once you receive insights that allow you to release Attachment to the worry and balance out the fear based data, it will no longer captivate your mind. You simply need the programing to balance out that which no longer serves you. You simply need programming that satisfies the need to upgrade the outdated programming so that a new version of Self can operate: a Self that is balanced, free of limiting beliefs and open to ALL possibilities. We are pleased with your understandings thus far. We will recommence in the next lesson with an understanding of your individual realities and how they affect the collective reality of your planet.

LESSON 19
THE COLLECTIVE MIND

Today, we are going to begin the process of explaining what has been referred to by many as the Collective Consciousness. Or as we prefer to call it – the Collective Mind. What is the Collective Mind exactly? Well, best understood, it is literally the "Community Mind," which is comprised of all data collected, from every thought EVER produced, from every being that has EVER existed on the planet. The Collective Mind houses billions upon billions of units of data, which runs the Planetary Program based on the collective intentions and creations of every single individual inhabitant of Earth. This Collective Mind allows all beings to co-exist on the same planet as part of the Global experience while simultaneously producing personal experiences based on each being's individual points of attraction. Seeing as you do co-exist, it is essential that your own personal experiences be tangible and observable by others so that your observable experiences are likewise considered a point of attraction of said observers. Because you co-exist at one time on the planet, living lives that tend to collide with each other, this Collective Mind was necessary to orchestrate the divine experience. It has become a most useful tool in showing the attraction of the

171

masses on a larger scale, which, when analyzed and understood correctly, perfectly demonstrates the current points of attraction of the individual.

To further expand upon the workings of the Collective Mind, it is important to understand that there exists the one Collective Mind, but within that mind are housed smaller factions of collectives such as towns, cities, nations, etc. All of which are beings and their thoughts of similar intentions that have come together to co-exist in one communal experience. These factions may seem to stand alone, but in reality, they exist as the one Collective Mind and serve the greater purpose of ALL. Such is the same concept in communal consciousness beyond physical form – this is merely a physical world manifestation to mirror that which is above.

Now, if you study your media and your history records, you will clearly see evidence of large scale displays of these individual points of attraction. These events may appear to be produced by individual factions, as opposed to global attraction, but the truth is that all that occurs is for the growth and expansion of the ALL. Wars, famines, periods of darkness, poverty, destruction are all large scale manifestations offering periods of rapid growth for humanity. Let us explain what we mean by this. It is during, and more specifically following, these periods that factions of mankind perform large scale transmutations of that which no longer serves them. It is not to say that these situations do not manifest again, due to limiting beliefs wearing a "different mask"; but what is evident from these experiences is that the Collective Mind brings its Self to a point of attraction that results in these "unwanted things," and then as a result of said unwanted things, the Collective pulls themselves out of the situation by collectively redirecting their attraction.

Let us look at a war for example. It is not necessary to look at a particular war – using war in general will suffice. When we study the instigation of wars and the events that cause most large scale conflict, there are a few things that are evident. Firstly, you have a government or leader riddled with insecurity. Leaders who lack personal power and Universal Truths, which result in their own insecurities – and clear lack of true power – acting out against another in an attempt to dominate or else be dominated is a mindset that has been practiced as "human nature" for ages. Secondly, you also have the masses who are so suppressed in their own power that they simply allow themselves to be controlled by their leaders. Leaders who have decided that they think it is best that those who live to serve them, run off to war to aid their insecurities. It is a very perplexing concept that the masses, who far outnumber the leaders and government officials, would so willingly offer their own lives in order to please the individual perspectives of a few. These men, who send others off to war, do not fight themselves as there is no need. They have others who have willingly given up their own power, those who have forgotten their ability to consciously create and experience the world they truly desire. So many would argue with the fact that it is often "required" to go to war: it is law. But in reality, these situations are merely a physical manifestation of the collective's denial of their own power. These are large scale manifestations, portraying numerous individuals who have forgotten their true power and the true nature of their existence. This can often be a difficult concept for people to accept, but in order to ascend beyond a "normal" physical mindset, ALL situations must be analyzed and understood from a nonphysical perspective. We must address the root of these issues to truly see past the illusions and limitations of the physical world.

Now understand when we say this: in reality, all that occurs, occurs as it is meant to. In actuality, many of the beings that partake in these events never intend to awaken to who they truly are. It simply isn't part of their current path to do so. And in saying this, it is so important to remember that all beings who have perished in past events have not died in vain, but rather served a most important function of assisting in the needs of the collective. Let us explain further how these war based events lead to growth, expansion and an opportunity for the progression of mankind.

When a war comes to an end, what is it that happens exactly? Do the officials decide to call off the war? In some cases, yes; but in most cases, that is not exactly what occurs. In reality, one side is defeated or willingly retreats. One side always "loses." Now why is this understanding important? This logic is essential to comprehending why a situation, such as war, offers growth and expansion, and how the collective thought patterns and mindset resulted in the conclusion. On one side, you have those that are dominant, who have seen their intentions through so that they may find themselves victorious. Then there are those who are on the receiving end of what is a perceived loss. But is it really a loss? Although it may appear to be a loss from a physical perspective, these beings have simply surrendered on a higher level. Let us explain further. These beings that have collectively "lost" the war have played a most important part.

Their own uncertainties and unwillingness to dominate resulted in the end of a power struggle. Although they may appear to be the losers, they are those that chose to give in, in an attempt to find peace. They are those that chose to surrender the thoughts of violence and war and shift their attention elsewhere. As a result, some choose to depart the physical world and find peace in the afterlife, whereas others choose to shift their attention to thoughts of submission and produce a different physical path than what has currently been attracted. Submission may seem to be a dangerous thought, but is it really? Is letting go of that which no longer serves you a bad thing? Is choosing to no longer fight, and instead select a different route to experience, not a necessary step for growth?

When this occurs; when the collective of this faction decides that it is time to retreat and allow a loss, there are multiple things that take place. The dominators or "winners" often proceed to stake their claim over the other, but more importantly, they proceed to carry on with their new mindset. They proceed to move on as victorious beings, empowered and eager for the next battle. Those that were perceived as being "the losers" then find themselves in the "shameful category," the category of the oppressed and defeated. Now let us examine what new paradigm has been created out of this situation.

We have two opposing and yet similar situations. We have one side who is empowered and another who is stripped of their power, but what is the similarity present? The intention. The intention is very much related. You have one side that has chosen to embrace their power and allowed a win, and you have another that has embraced their power and allowed a loss.

There is in reality no difference between the two. The win is not really a win and the loss is not really a loss; both are merely points of attraction, merely a choice made between the Collective Minds. There is in reality no difference between both sides, and all is but a choice. This choice is what drives the collective. All wars, and again we mean all wars, present the choice of a "loss" or "win," but in reality, it is not the title that is achieved that is important, it is the choice that is made by the collective. The bottom line is that for a loss or win to occur, it must be the will of the Collective; however, from a bigger perspective, no one has really won or lost anything. All are precisely where they should be. All are simply playing the role they were meant to, which was necessary for individual and ultimately planetary growth and expansion. This perceived win or loss is in reality neither good nor bad, both experiences are simply what IS and a physical representation of a chosen point of attraction. ALL aspects of these war based experiences indicate a Higher Self chosen path, necessary for desired growth and expansion!

The Collective Mindset chooses who will be the perceived winner and the loser. The Collective Mindset chooses who will be the dominators or the dominated. What determines how the collective will choose? Individual lives and programming, essentially. And how does this really factor into what we are saying? Simply put, those that are "good" at dominating and those that are "good" at being dominated are designed to do so. They have been programmed by their own "cultures" to play these roles. Now, let us address what happens when these "roles" – of the dominator and dominated – begin a pattern of repeated manifestation. In every case, you will of course find your wars and you will likewise find your defeats.

But those that are continually defeated will have learned from each experience and with each successive manifestation of defeat, are presented with choices to further their individual and collective experiences. They can choose to stay as the oppressed, or they can choose to move on to play a new role. This can often lead to the rebuilding of a nation, into a more peaceful nation; but in many cases, this can lead to a simple role reversal of the dominated wanting to become the dominator, as is evident by your last world war.

The fact is, these wars present the opportunity for growth and expansion for both parties. Let us likewise address the growth and expansion of the nations that are bred for war and bred for conflict. These nations will too find themselves presented with choices. The collective of these nations will continue on the path that they have been bred for, until they collectively decide they wish to be free of the experience and desire something new. Even the greatest conquerors must one day decide to step aside and chase a new dream. There is only so much to be conquered and eventually the thrill will be lost – from a nonphysical perspective. These people who have been bred for this role will eventually reach a point where these actions no longer serve them.

Examples of large scale physical manifestations exist to show the collective what their cultural programming has bred them to do or, essentially, what their collective cultural data has resulted in. Current generations and future generations will assess these actions, as one's "history," and determine what route is desired moving forward. In the case of war, your species has progressed leaps and bounds by realizing that both domination and oppression do not create desired results, and that equality and allowance of personal beliefs creates the most peaceful scenario. No way is the right way – all ways are the right way!

It is most important to understand that because you co-exist together, because you choose to experience this life in groups and in cultural families, you are presented with large scale manifestations. This allows you to perceive physical examples of your collective programming, to study and analyze, so that collectively you can choose new experiences for growth and expansion. This programming can be analyzed in your local community, your state, your country and on a global scale. You can analyze the past actions of any small town or an entire country to see the evolutions in consciousness that took place as a result of their actions. You can see how one choice stems another and another, and how as the individual mind acquires more freedom, personal independence and power, the intentions of the nation, as a whole, shift. These global events that you see are nothing more than an opportunity to address programming that needs to be upgraded. When the programming is updated, firstly on an individual bases, the Collective Mind will then be equipped with the essential data to run an upgraded version of the Planetary Mind and all unwanted wars and disease will cease to exist. All will be operating a version of Self that is focused more on individual happiness: a precursor that is required, not to become "selfish," but to take your focus off of condemning what others are doing. When you focus on your own affairs, knowing that your happiness is key, you would never allow another's beliefs or actions to affect your own well-being. You would focus on and protect your own interest, not in an attempt to disregard another; but you would do so knowing that you need not focus on another's choices, as you know that only you can truly bring your Self happiness. You would not concern your Self with what brings another happiness, as it is only what brings YOU happiness that is important to you.

This may seem to be such a selfish way of acting, but we assure you that this is the opposite of selfish. By tending to your own personal mind – by choosing happiness for you and focusing on your own personal growth – you contribute something far greater to the Collective Mind than the path of attempting to control and reform others to your way of thinking. You contribute peace and allowance into the Collective Mind, and if all where to do the same, the world would know peace. That is all for now. We will recommence in the next lesson with an expanded understanding of your role in the Collective Mind.

LESSON 20
YOUR ROLE IN THE COLLECTIVE

In today's lesson, we will continue sharing our perspectives on the Collective Mind so that you may begin to understand your part in All That Is and in doing so, assist the entire world. As a Lightworker, you are responsible for your existence only. You cannot force another to do something they do not want to, and you cannot make something "better" for another, as much as you might desire to do so. Your role as a Lightworker is to assist the world on its path to Ascension, but your actual function may not fully be understood by you at this time. Because it is in your nature to believe that you are to fully devote your Self to the cause, as you have done in previous lives, you often step into a role of martyrdom. You are not sure why you feel this way or what exactly it is you are supposed to do, but you embark upon your role as a Lightworker thinking that it will be hard and require a lot of sacrifice and dedication on your part. You take this role on with great pride but also with a sense of weariness.

As we have explained in previous lessons, this is but a limiting belief carrying forward, and it is nothing to do be concerned about. This is your nature, but what we want to impress upon you today is the Truth of your role in this life.

You are not here to sacrifice Self. You are not here to toil at the expense of making others happy. You are here in this life to experience what brings you Joy. Although we say this, many of you will still not understand. **Moving forward in this life, you are not required to experience anything other than Joy!** Now in saying this, let us explain. Regardless of your role as a Lightworker, you are not here to do anything that does not bring you true Joy and bliss. You are not to take on another student or client when you have reached capacity simply because you feel that you should. You are not to work two shifts to help others simply because you believe that is what a Lightworker should do. You are not to sacrifice your own health, well-being or Self-interest at any cost.

Let us explain why. When you first hear this, your natural reaction as a Lightworker is to tense up – to pull back. You feel that it is selfish to tell someone no when they are asking for assistance. Many feel that as a Lightworker they are supposed to help anyone and everyone, whenever they ask, regardless of the consequences for Self. To this we say: who says? Who wrote this list of requirements on how you should act? We have not seen such a list. As we have said many times, there is no one way – there is only the way that works for you. You do not need to care about what another is doing that makes them believe they are holy. It does not matter what a religion says or what a spiritual person you admire says. If it does not resonate with you, it is not the way for you. The way for others is not necessarily your way, and only YOU know your way. And so let us stress again: you are not to do anything that you do not desire to do. We say this simply because the process will be tainted with limiting beliefs and you will not be allowing your Self the opportunity to create your Heaven on Earth. Now, why is this concept of creating your Heaven on Earth so important, you might wonder?

Well, friends, you must understand, and you must fully embrace WHY you are here. You are here to create your Heaven on Earth. You are here to shift the data in the Collective Mind. As you awaken to who you are and as you add new data that is in alignment with Authentic Self, you will begin to allow the Collective Mind to operate a new version of Earth 2.0. But this will only occur if the data is accurate and genuine. There is no need to try to fool anyone, or your Self more importantly, by pretending to be the "spiritual being" whom you have been told you should be. There is no need to help another out of obligation, because in doing so, you will be providing more data to the collective that is not genuine or in alignment with the purpose of your incarnation. As an Advocate of Truth, you are here to set an example of living Heaven on Earth. You are here to show others that the world they exist in is not as it appears and that in reality there is so much more to the story. You are here to show the world that you are ALL Divine Creators and that everyone who desires to do so can follow suit. You are here to show the world the great illusion that exists, and in doing so, you are going to change the Collective Mind and usher in true peace on Earth. You will not achieve this by doing things you do not want to do; you will not do this by putting on a mask and trying to be something you are not, and you will most certainly not achieve this by trying to live someone else's version of Heaven on Earth. You are to be YOU – you are to live YOUR dream. If you do not want to do something, do not do it. Only do what brings you Joy. ALWAYS.

There is no set in stone or definite rulebook when it comes to being a Lightworker, this is most true; however, we believe there is one "rule" that should exist for all Lightworkers: **ALWAYS EXIST IN JOY.** It is only through setting your Joyous example and shining your light that the rest of the world will awaken and ascend. Let us look at it this way: where would you be now if you did not have the examples set forth by other great inventors, innovators and visionaries? If you did not have their examples to show you greater truths, mankind would never move forward. These people show the world proof of All That Is. They provide tangible evidence to appease the mind in the reprogramming process so that you may remember who you truly are. They are the cure to the "Physical World Mindset," and without them, you would not be able to quiet the programming that tells you, you can't. Without them, you would not see the physical proof you needed to accept that another way exists. They show the world that there is so much more to reality than there appears to be, and they show others just how truly powerful each individual is. They set an example of the unlimited potential and power that resides within ALL, and they guide others to see this truth within themselves. Without the way showers, without the great examples, the world would never change.

You are not here to set an example of a mediocre life. You are not here to live your "so-so" Heaven on Earth. You are here to live the best possible version of your life that you could possibly imagine. You are here to live the optimal state of grace in physicality. This may seem like a hopeless dream, but we assure you, this is your destiny. So please remember, dearest brothers and sisters, follow YOUR Joy. Do not do something because you have this false notion in your head that you have to. Do what feels Joyous to you; do what makes your heart sing. And we assure you in doing so, you will be assisting the world in the most optimal way. Do NOT willingly allow your power to be taken away by half-heartedly doing what others have told you to do. If something does not resonate with you, this is an indication that it is not your path to follow. If what one teaches does resonates with you, this is most wonderful, but find the variation of the practice that works for you. Find the version that suits your needs and your interests, and do not be afraid to write your own version of the story! So please remember the one and only rule we offer to you: ALWAYS follow your own path and seek your own Joy – ALWAYS.

We want you to understand that the time of martyrdom is over. The time of believing that another's emotional state and needs are more important than yours MUST pass, or you will not fulfill your function. It is time to realize that you are not here to "serve" anyone – other than your Self. You are not to deny your Self rest or an opportunity to experience something desired simply because you think you must help another at your expense. There is no need to deny what Self needs, and in doing so, provide a false example of Joy to others. You are not to develop a savior complex, thinking that it is your job to save everyone and failing to see that no one needs to be saved from the path they have chosen for growth and expansion! No, it is not for you to create their happiness, it is for you to create YOURS and in doing so, provide an optimal example to those that you assist! For you see, dearest one, those that you assist have only been drawn to you for the tangible example and, ultimately, reprogramming data that you can provide, which they need to assist them on their path! You are not responsible for anything other than providing the example you promised you would when you came forth with the intention to serve as an Advocate of Truth.

You alone are responsible for your growth and expansion, as all those that come to you for assistance are responsible for their own. You serve the world best by eradicating the limiting belief of Self-Sacrifice and a life of disadvantage for those that choose the path of healers/teachers. You serve the world best by showing others that ALL deserve abundance, all deserve happiness, and all deserve a life of true Joy and bliss. A life of balance, consisting of Self Care first, followed by the care of others. A life of Self-interest, with the sole intention to provide the optimal example of true Self Love and Joy for ALL.

Now please understand, we are in no way saying do not assist your brothers and sisters! What we are saying is to assist when it feels Joyous and when assisting is truly desired by Self. Do not assist out of obligation and guilt. You are not responsible for creating the happiness of others, and regardless of how much they may protest, you are not asked to do everything for anyone else. You are only to serve you, and you are to love and appreciate you enough so that you may then – Joyfully and truly – offer loving assistance to others. There will be many times when you are called on for assistance, and with a new mindset of caring for Self first, you will realize just how much more you are able to help others. Just how much more you are willing to give of your Self, when you do not feel you have anything to lose or give up in the process.

We adore this time with you, and today, we want you to realize how special you really are: how important and necessary you are. You will change this world. In fact, you have already begun to. That is all for now. We will recommence in the next lesson with the first of many essential teachings on how to create your Heaven on Earth.

LESSON 21
NO LIMITS

What is meant when we say – Create Your Heaven on Earth? What is it that we really mean by this statement? So many of you will read these words and begin to imagine a life where you find your Self in conditions and situations different from what you currently perceive. Even if you are pleased with a large portion of your life, there will undoubtedly be a change – in some form or another – that you could imagine to "improve" your life. Now, we want you to take a moment to dwell on what it is you imagine would transform your life into your own version of Heaven. We want you to examine this superior reality you have created in your mind, and we want to ask you – is this the best you can come up with?

Today, we want to emphasis what we really mean by creating your Heaven on Earth. Today, we want to show you that this statement does not mean creating the world you have been told should exist for you. It does not imply creating a mediocre existence based on what you currently think is possible either. And finally, it most certainly does not denote creating a limited reality based on what you believe you do or do not deserve. NO, creating your Heaven on Earth means creating the most optimal and the most exceptional life one could possibly imagine for themselves. There is nothing too big, there is nothing too grand that it cannot be obtained. There are no limits and we mean NO LIMITS. So many of you will see these words, and yet you will still offer some form of resistance thinking thoughts like: "Well, maybe that is the case, but what I want might be selfish of me to want or just too unrealistic to achieve. What I want might be the one instance where this is not so because I really don't deserve to have what I truly desire. Why should I have these things when others do not?" To this we say, these are but limiting beliefs. Anything and everything, regardless of the perceived size or grandeur of the creation, EVERYTHING is possible and is your birthright to have. There is nothing that is out of reach for you. Nothing. This is what you must fully embrace. There is no dream to big and no task too great that it cannot be achieved. Please remember this, and you will allow the creation process to run that more efficiently.

Let us address again what is meant when we say creating your Heaven on Earth. Simply put, this means creating the best possible experiences that you can. Keep in mind, as you grow and expand, your desired experiences will continuously adapt with your growth and expansion. So remember, you are not to worry about what you are going to want ten years from now; you are to focus on what you desire now. You are to focus on the optimal desire NOW. Do not be concerned about what others have told you is possible. For as we have explained, it is your duty as a Lightworker to set your example and shine your light so that you may show others the Truth of their existence. It is your duty as a Lightworker to bring forth the Truths of the nature of man so that others may follow in your footsteps and ultimately create a world in the image of peace and tranquillity. It is only through finding your own personal Heaven on Earth that you will achieve this. Why, you might ask? Well, it is only through understanding that each is responsible for their own existence that the world will do away with the need to compete.

Imagine a world where one does not feel threatened by the possessions of another. A world where one does not feel that there is not enough to go around, and where one understands that if he enjoys the creation of another, he can simply desire it for himself and see that it is done. Imagine a world with no wars, no greed and no hatred. A world where all had what they desired, without hording possessions purely out of the fear of another staking their claim on what is available. All would have what they desired. All would be happy and have precisely what they need and want – indefinitely. This would be utopia, but to create this, Lightworker, you must first create your own version of Heaven on Earth. In doing so, you will show others that they too can achieve these things, and through you, a mighty light will embrace the planet, and the world will know peace.

So how does one do this, you ask? How does one begin to create their Heaven on Earth? How does one truly release all limitations and step into their power – to allow themselves to create as they were divinely fashioned to do so? We will teach you, of course. There have been many teachings created on your planet. There have been many messages channelled and many books written on this subject. These are most marvelous tools that have assisted many in awakening to their natural ability to create, but the lessons we have written will be different. The lessons we have written are meant to serve those with a particular type of programming. These lessons will serve the much needed purpose of filling a gap within the Collective knowledge and will provide the tangible data needed for you, and others like you, to move forward. As a result, Lightworkers of a new and never before seen collection of programming will be able to receive what is needed to move forward in their own growth and expansion and ultimately Global Purpose. Allow us to explain further.

There have been many teachings that have assisted those of specific phases or specific divisions of Lightworkers, if you will. But now there are others – others who came forward at a time of great change. A time when the collective was shifting and a time where great contrast occurred. Beings like this channel, who chose to incarnate into frequently uncomfortable and undesirable life situations so that they would then be able to recognize the change that was needed. These beings chose to come forth into experiences that would seem very undesirable to many, but experiences that were extremely necessary to reach this particular point in time. As a result of these upbringings and as a result of the copious amounts of inauthentic data collected throughout their young lives, these beings have, shall we say, more difficult data to overcome. This is precisely why you are reading this book. You are one of these beings that has this data that can only be overcome with a certain type of reprogramming. You have data that requires a new type of reprogramming that has not yet been translated into physical words until now.

We will offer new approaches and new techniques, not because they are superior to any other wonderful and most marvelous method, but because they are what is required for your specific programming, what is needed to assist those of your particular consciousness. You see, you, and all those like you, came to bring about change. You were the pioneers and the advocates for the creation of a new world, from the very beginning. Many of you have seen great turmoil in your days, but this is where it ends. This is where you step into your power, where you embrace who you are and why you are here. Today is the day you leave it all behind and walk onward into the new world. Today is the day you choose FREEDOM!

And so we ask you to remember that these teachings are in no way better than any other teachings; they are in no way superior to any other methods that you enjoy. These lessons are simply what is required for the beings who chose to incarnate at this particular time, to serve a particular function. These lessons have been called forth by a collective of beings so that they may receive the necessary tools to move forward and embrace who they truly are. Remember, this is simply the way that works for you, and in reality, all ways are the right way.

Let us move forward in this lesson with a practical understanding of how to create your Heaven on Earth. We will begin with further explanation of the Universal Truths and then offer you an exercise to perform. As we have always said, Joy is the answer to everything. Joy is what you must seek, as Joy is your natural state of being. Joy is the very essence of who you are outside of physical existence, and so you must first and foremost remember to do that, and only that, which brings you Joy.

191

Second, you must remember that ALL experiences are essential. They are but stepping stones to get you where you will be. So, if we start this process and you do not find the results you are expecting, you must remember that this is only happening in an attempt to show you the path that must be taken to get where you desire to be. If you do not see the validations you were expecting, it is simply because you have not created as you intended to create. It is because your thoughts have not produced what you say you intended for them to produce, and your physical reality is simply reflecting the true intentions of your thoughts. Please remember as we move forward to not fight against ANYTHING. Do not be hard on your Self thinking that you have failed. Every step is an essential step, and every creation is attempting to show you what must be adapted or what can simply be maintained. This is where we will proceed now, with further understandings of the Two Methods of Creation.

We have extensively covered understandings on Transmute & Initiate, and by now, you should understand what is to be achieved by this method. We believe that it should be clear by now how essential transmutation is, and how this is the means by which one can initiate a new creation on the physical plane. We are so pleased with your understandings thus far, but as always, there is so much more to learn. As we have indicated in a previous lesson, the process of transmutation is simply changing the form, or in the sense of creation, changing your point of attraction. Now what exactly is meant by this? In the creation process, you are always, at every moment of every day, bringing your Self into alignment with that which is to exist in every subsequent moment. You are always directing your thoughts to that which you choose to experience moving forward. Now let us expand on this further. Throughout your day, you are always continuously creating with every thought and every ounce of resistance you offer. As we have indicated in a previous lesson, your natural state of being is a continual flow of well-being. It is only your resistant thoughts and programming that essentially blocks this well-being and manipulates this optimal vibration, which then manifests onto the physical plane as the "best" version based on what your mind would allow. This concept is what we will address now. We will delve into an understanding of how your thoughts are actually creating your reality so that you may fully grasp the importance of mental transmutation.

This concept of your thoughts creating your reality is not new to you and is a concept that many have come to embrace. But in the remainder of these lessons, we intend to delve much deeper into this Truth so that optimal understandings may be achieved. It is always the goal of Source Energy for you to receive the best possible resources for Self, at every moment. The intention is never to receive anything less than optimal Joyful experiences, but due to your programming, Self offers resistance which then creates a varying degree of the original optimal vibration. Let us expand on this using a monetary example. As each person's perspectives are unique, everyone's version of the best possible financial situation will be completely unique based on their own individual data. So in this respect, as there is no universal "perfect" amount of money or no universal "worst case" amount of money, it becomes evident that the varying degrees of vibration are simply a matter of perspective. This indicates that because each person's perception of what is considered to be "good" or "bad" about money is so contrasting, money therefore does not offer a universal good or bad dual concept. Let us explain further. For some, they believe less money is better, and for others, they believe more money is better – it is simply a matter of perspective. So what does this mean? This means that there is NO duality based concept for money. There is no good or bad amount, there is no right or wrong amount, there is no perfect or imperfect amount, and there are NO opposites in opposition. There are simply a million varying degrees of the same vibration, simply varying choices and unlimited possibilities for the financial flow that you choose to allow! So from this perspective, we can then examine the essential understanding of Neutrality in the creation process. Neutrality is an understanding that must be achieved in order for one to fully grasp the Reality Creation Process and remove all Attachments, to all physical form creations. To be a Conscious Creator, you MUST learn to practice Neutrality – not Duality.

Achieving a state of Neutrality is coming to an understanding that all creations are equal and do not favor either opposing sides of Duality. All creations are Neutral and are neither good nor bad. For example: having more money is not better than having no money and vice versa. The creation of more money, or simply put – manifesting a pile of cash – is not a "higher" vibrational frequency manifestation, as many of you believe. Many of you look at your desired financial state and think, "Okay, I need to raise my vibration to become a vibrational match to this wonderful awesome pile of cash, as it is the best vibration available to me now and I desire it." To this we say that you are looking at it incorrectly. Having a pile of cash or having no pile of cash is precisely the same in terms of the "level" of vibration. One is not higher or "better" than the other. Both are neutral and simply varying degrees of the same Universal Source Energy. We prefer to look at it as a scale that moves horizontally as opposed to vertically. Having more money is not at the top of the scale and less money at the bottom. You simply have your horizontal scale and varying degrees of numerous possibilities of financial allowance exists all over the scale on a neutral level. These represent the varying degrees of the One Universal Vibration. One is not better than the other as they all stem from the same Source. So many of you look at your creations thinking that what you no longer desire is below that which you desire. You think you must raise your vibration to match this "superior creation," and this is one of the primary limiting beliefs of the Conscious Reality Creation process. What you want is precisely the same as what you say you do not want. They are both resources produced from the same vibration and merely represent varying degrees of the One. They are both nothing more than resources to get you to the experience you desire.

We wish for you today to practice an exercise. We wish for you to look at what you have around you and then imagine what it is that you desire moving forward. We want you to analyze why the unwanted is different from the wanted. Let us use the monetary example again, as so many of you are currently working on manifesting your ideal version of this creation. If you are not concerned with dollars, let us use the same scenario on what it is that you are currently trying to manifest: be it a relationship, a desired body image or a career. Simply adjust the instructions to suit your needs.

We recommend that you use a piece of paper to write down the answers to this exercise. We encourage you to note and acknowledge all that enters your mind so that we can achieve an optimal analysis.

Look at the number in your bank account and then imagine the number you wish to see. We want you to examine what the difference is between the money you have and the money you want. Is there any real difference between the two creations, when viewing them beyond the obvious physical opposites of not enough and enough? Analyze how having more in your bank account, as opposed to less, would add more value to your life? What would be "better" about having more dollars in your account? We want you to analyze what it is that you desire about having more money in your account and we want you to pay attention to the feeling. We want you to pay attention to the emotions that are triggered when you focus on what is currently in your account and what you desire to have in your account. We want you to take note of any and all limiting beliefs that come forward, and we want you to note any and all thoughts that offer resistance. Do not rush this analysis, and feel free to spend as much time as needed pondering these questions.

We will recommence in the next lesson with our analysis of the findings.

LESSON 22
RELEASING ATTACHMENT

We will begin this lesson with a brief recap of what we have learned thus far. By now you should fully understand your purpose for incarnation. You should have begun to realize how essential it is to work on Self, and create an ideal reality for Self, so that you may provide an optimal example for others. You should understand the basic process of Reality Creation and how it is essential to first Transmute in order to Initiate the allowance of a desired creation on the physical plane. You should fully understand why it is so essential that you begin today, transmuting all that no longer serves you, and you should fully embrace your birthright to have all that you desire. Allow us now to pick up where we left off.

We are pleased with your understandings thus far, and we are eager to broaden your perspectives by addressing the various limiting beliefs associated with Reality Creation. In us doing so, you will receive the necessary programming to allow the opportunity for the transmutation of all that does not serve you. We will give you new perspectives to bring to light the heart of these beliefs, and we will provide new data so that you can essentially run a new program: a program that will allow you to finally succeed at deliberate Reality Creation. Let us now address the exercise that was proposed in the previous lesson. Let us now examine the results of this exercise. What we find when this exercise is performed is that so many of you experience one of two things.

ONE: You were so consumed by the sense of panic that ensued as a result of you first focusing on that which you are currently attracting, that you were unable to allow your Self to experience the vibration of any other option.

~OR~

TWO: You tended toward simply running away from and ignoring what you do not want all together and merely projected your Self into the desired future you seek, daydreaming about how wonderful it will be. We want to discuss both of these scenarios.

Let us discuss the first scenario. When faced with something that you are very emotionally tied to, you often find it difficult to shift your attention from that which you say you do not want. You began this exercise focusing upon what you do not want and then found that you began a spiral of fear based projections – projections that will ultimately create more of the experiences you do not want. Why is it that this occurs? Why is it that you are unable to shift your attention from that which you say you do not want? Well, it is your Attachment to that which you say you no longer want.

Now let us address the second scenario. If you chose this route, you had no problem ignoring the creation in your current experience. You simply chose to direct your attention to what you desire, believing that life will be "better" once you achieve that which you desire. Although this may be what you have currently surmised from alternate Reality Creation teachings, we assure you this as well will not produce what you desire. Again, what is the problem that exists here? Again, it is Attachment! In both cases you are attached to your creations. On the one hand, you are attached to the "bad" unwanted, and on the other hand, you are attached to the "good" wanted. In both scenarios, Self is presented with the opportunity for transmutation, but instead you are choosing to keep your Self tied to that which you say you do not want.

In the first scenario it should be quite obvious how you will continue to attract more of what you currently have, but let us expand upon the second. Why is it that this will not yield the desired results? Well, it is partly because of your projection of what is desired and partly because of your fear based need to avoid what exists in your current experience. Allow us to explain further. You are not choosing your creation now, because you are establishing "conditions" for your creation to be allowed. You believe you are simply indicating that when you do choose to allow that which you desire life will be better. But what you are truly intending is that your creation cannot come until life is "better." It is this fantasy of believing that life will be "better" someday that traps you, as it is insinuating distaste for what you are currently experiencing – thus, creating Attachment. You fail to see that your projection of a "better" life will never come to be because you are attached to what you have now.

199

You only project as a means to escape from what you have now, and by definition this intention is fear based and will always keep you tied to what you say you do not want.

If you did not have fear for what currently exists in your experience, you would not feel the need to run from it and create these fantasies about a "better" life. There would be no need to run, there would only be acceptance of What Is and what has been attracted for growth and expansion. If you did not have fear, you would feel gratitude for every stepping stone upon your path. You would perceive them as necessary requirements to keep you moving forward, and you most certainly would not try to run and hide from them. If you find your Self consumed with fear of your creations to any degree, you are practicing Attachment, and you will not achieve the physical manifestations of the resources you desire.

Now let us make one thing very clear, you are not to pretend that you are pleased and Joyous about your current experience. Instead, you are to practice Non-Attachment to your current experience and the manifestations within it simply for the purpose of allowing transmutation. And how is this achieved? Simply by understanding the Neutrality of all physical plane creations. For you must come to see that a Conscious Creator cannot flourish in a world of Duality; in fact, conscious creation is not possible in a world of such restrictions. Living within a world of Duality, of opposites in opposition and a constant struggle between what is wanted and unwanted, creates a situation where deliberate choice is impossible. In order to understand why this is, you must come to truly understand the intention behind Conscious Reality Creation vs. Duality based thinking.

From a Duality based mindset, one perceives opposition and struggle – NOT choice. One perceives the bad creation as a forced reality and the good creation as the wanted alternative to escape the "bad."

Whereas the intention behind Conscious Realty Creation implies the knowing of choice. It implies that the Creator sees past the illusion of one creation being bad and another being good, and they most certainly see past the illusion of a struggle between the two. A Conscious Creator understands that there is no struggle to keep the good and avoid the bad, because they understand choice! They understand that ALL is choice. And if this is the Truth, then no creation can be deemed bad and no creation can be deemed good or better, as all is simply one's choice for growth and expansion.

If the fear surrounding this option of Duality and the possibility of a "bad" creation ceased to exist, then one would see that choice is all there is. This is precisely how a Conscious Creator must operate. They must see past the Fear of Failure laced within this Duality based thinking. They must understand that failure is not an option, as Law states that all must be as was intended. And so a Conscious Creator must have no fear of a possible "bad" creation and must only see choice – what is desired and what is intended, as what will be. A Conscious Creator would never doubt achieving what is desired simply because of an available opposite choice. For the Conscious Creator knows that this alternative is simply that – a possible alternative choice. Knowing that the choice is theirs, a Conscious Creator will always choose resources that Joyously serve them in all of their experiences. They see

201

beyond the illusion of Duality and the illusory struggle between alternate possibilities, as the perception of a struggle is not conceivable when the Fear of Failure is eliminated. Why would one fear or even acknowledge the "bad" if they know that they do not have to choose the bad? If one accepts their ability to choose and have what is desired, does the opposing alternative not cease to exist all together? Such is the process of thinking for the elimination of the Duality based mindset! A process of logical thinking that you must master in order to become a Conscious Creator!

So know this: if you want to become a Conscious Creator, if you want to hold the scepter of power, YOU MUST see past the fear and struggle presented by Duality. You must see Duality for what it is: simply a means to experience the light and dark for growth and expansion. A necessary illusion created as a means to experience the great "test" in an authentic testing grounds! It is not bad – it is most certainly necessary – BUT the illusion of it must be overcome to move forward and supersede the manifestations produced, as a result of it. Release the fear; release the illusion of opposites in opposition, and embrace the Neutrality of ALL That Is!

Let us now proceed to further explain what is meant by Neutrality. To begin to comprehend this concept, you must first come to truly understand all of your creations. Although your mind may perceive that you have wanted and unwanted creations, in reality, there is no such thing. There is always only wanted experiences for growth and expansion. There is always only the by-product of your thoughts that create the wanted experiences. Now many of you would still argue that you do not want the perceived "bad" things that happen to you, but we assure you, you indicate your wanting of them by your attention to them. Once you eliminate your attachment to them, by no longer perceiving them as "bad" and unwanted, you will then release your attraction of them. You must come to see that there is always only WANTED experiences! Allow us to further expand on this most important understanding.

As we have indicated in previous lessons, you are not your body or mind. The True You is the Higher Aspect of you, and you are not defined by the physical world programming that has created the "personality" that is "you." So what does this mean? Remember what we have taught you: all experiences were a necessary part of your growth and expansion. All experiences are required and essential to get you where you are now and to get you where you will be. EVERY experience. From this perspective, you can see how even the perceived unwanted creations were in fact wanted by the True You to allow you to reach this very moment. All the creations in your current experience and all your creations to come are essential and ARE WANTED. So it is time that you take accountability for YOUR creations. Understand that on a Soul level, you have chosen these creations to assist you on your path, and understand from a physical perspective that you have indicated that you in fact desired these experiences by your attention to them – whether you say you intended to or not. You are the one calling the shots here. Remember that. You are not defined by your circumstances, you define your circumstances. Today, it is time to stop the statements that suggest that life has been unfair to you because we assure this is not the case. All creations are wanted by you, for you.

So now, let us return back to this concept of Neutrality. Now that you fully acknowledge that all creations are wanted, let us again discuss the Neutrality of all creations in existence. As we touched upon in the previous lesson, all creations exist upon the same level. There is not a creation that you desire that is a "higher vibration" or a "better" creation then another simply because you desire to experience it. As we indicated previously, what is considered good or bad and wanted or unwanted is simply a matter of perspective and the by-product of a Duality based mindset. There are no universal labels for creations, and so all creations simply are and represent varying degrees of the same vibration. Figuratively speaking, these creations exist on a horizontal scale with the various degrees presented before you. It is not more difficult for you to choose one degree over the other, as they are all on the same level, and one is just as easily assessable as the other. Whether you choose to believe it is difficult is all a matter of perception.

What plagues most of you in the Reality Creation Process is your Attachment to your creations. Your fear based desire for what you wish to experience clouds you from seeing that you are keeping what is desired away from you by being attached to it. By desiring a creation for any reason other than your choice to have it, you produce an opposite in opposition that will appear to be the dreadful and "painful reality." By believing that things will get "better" once you receive that which you desire, you are whole heartedly implying your aversion to what you currently have. Now again let us stress, we are not here to tell you that you must pretend that you enjoy what you currently have. We are not even telling you that you have to somehow try to find happiness with your current attractions. No, that is not what we will tell you at all. We are simply telling you that you have to release the Attachment to both the PERCEIVED wanted and unwanted. You must let go of the illusion of the Good vs. Bad Duality mindset and you must come to see that all creations are wanted and all creations are necessary. You have to come to accept all creations for what they are: simply neutral resources. Resources that are determined based on choice. One is not better than the other, and all are on an equal level for you to choose from so that you may have exactly what you desire for growth and expansion. When you understand this, you will emerge as a Conscious Creator in the Reality Creation Process, and you will be ready to create only that which brings you Joy. You will have superseded the need for creations that were necessary for growth and expansion to overcome Duality, and you will be ready to create your Heaven on Earth!

So many teachings on Reality Creation have taught you that you must simply find a way to appreciate what you have, and although we do not negate the value of these teachings, practicing this process has not and will not work for you. Your programming is different, and as a result, your mind functions in a different manner that will not allow these teachings to compute. You must switch your mindset from trying to force your Self to be pleased with what you have to a mindset that understands that what you have is merely a matter of choice. You must come to realize that all things that exist on the physical plane, be it people, animals and objects alike, are resources for individual and collective growth and expansion. They are resources that assist you on your path, and it is these resources that have even brought you to this point in time – so that you may now choose to be a Conscious Creator who is capable of choosing resources at will. Release the Attachment to the "unwanted" by recognizing the Neutrality of all creations and embracing that all that exists in your physical reality is merely a product of your current point of attraction. Release the Attachment to your "wanted" creations by understanding that ALL creations are wanted and all creations are simply an available resource that you are drawing to you, to experience desired growth and expansion. You must release Attachment to all physical creations in your life including other incarnated beings. Now, allow us to explain what we mean by this.

You are not to become "cold hearted." To the contrary. Releasing Attachment to things in the physical is not meant to allow you to detach from them spiritually, it is meant to allow you to detach from them Dualistically. When you are so emotionally tied to a resource that your "happiness" depends upon the existence of this creation, either in your current experience or your "future" reality, you will always find discomfort and deny your Self the experiences you truly desire. If you continue to cling to resources out of a sense of security, so that you may find a false sense of satisfaction and purpose, you will never move past what you say is unwanted. When you recognize these resources for what they are, you will be able to detach your Self from them, releasing any co-dependency you have established as a requirement for your happiness.

To demonstrate the effects of Attachment and the importance of detachment, let us use a relationship between two people as an example. Let us suppose that one has formed a strong

Attachment to the other, and this is causing severe discomfort in the relationship.

Like many in the physical world, the attached individual believes that their happiness is dependent on the other. So much so that they plan all of their future experiences around existing with this person. This mindset undoubtedly causes great discomfort when the thought enters their mind of not having this person in their future experiences. Why is this so painful? Simply because of the Attachment to this particular person. This individual's strong need for another to exist in their reality, simply to bring about a supposed state of happiness, prevents them from being able to see the truth: that happiness exists outside of this other person. People with strong Attachments to other physical beings fail to see that happiness is not dependent upon this being, but rather, happiness is dependent upon the inner workings of their mind. If peace and balance is maintained on the mental plane and happiness from a mental perspective is achieved, this will then manifest onto the physical plane as happy tangible experiences WITH this other being. But all must begin on the mental plane and mirror onto the physical, as form is simply the physical manifestation of intention. From this perspective, it becomes evident that forcing an individual into the role of the sole provider of happiness is a futile pursuit. For bringing about happiness is the sole obligation of the pursuer of happiness and does not fall upon that which is being pursued. Happiness will reflect in physical reality, once the pursuer allows said happiness to manifest onto the physical plane, via a clear intention and allowing state of mind.

Again, let us stress that we do not advocate that this person need pretend that they could be happy without this other person; what we are saying is that their Attachment to this person is preventing peace in their experiences. Let us explain further. Let us see this other person for what they truly are: a neutral resource available so that one may have desired experiences for growth and expansion. From this perspective, it becomes clear that it is simply choice that determines whether or not this other person exists in one's experience. It becomes evident that there are unlimited varying degrees of possible experiences with this individual, and it is simply choice that determines which degree is allowed. Your greatest hindrance in accepting these things is that you fail to see who you truly are and "who" it is that is choosing the resources that flow into your experiences.

When you come to understand that people and things are resources for your own personal growth, you release the Attachment of fearing that you will lose them and ultimately find your current and future experiences filled with dread and unhappiness. In often cases, when one finds themselves in a relationship based on Attachment, they are constantly creating projections of a future filled with dread and sadness without this person. As a result of this fearful mindset, many become so afraid of losing the resource they have created as a co-dependency for their happiness, that they essentially prevent themselves from enjoying their current experience with this other person. Consequently, this projection creates scenarios of discomfort, insecurities and great conflict that if not resolved will lead to the ending of the relationship. All of which was predictable and easily avoidable if the Attachment was properly understood and released.

It is important to note that in saying these things, we do accept that all occurs as it was meant to, in accordance with your highest good and the highest good of others. It is important to understand that all physical beings in your life will stay in your experiences as long as they are assisting with growth and expansion. Some will stay a lifetime and others will come and go when needed. The fact is all physical creations, including other physical beings, are simply resources bringing to you what is needed. You will likewise play the role of a resource for others, and throughout your life, you will serve the great function of assisting others in their growth and expansion, wandering in and out of others' lives when needed. You must accept the path of others and the path that has been laid before you, by you, for growth and expansion. You must not fear the loss of others, and instead, you must embrace what they have taught you. You must accept this, and in doing so, you will release Attachment.

This concept is precisely the same with all other physical creations. If you have a strong desire to obtain something in your future, but then live your moments in fear of never reaching said future, you will find great discomfort. If you cannot allow your Self to see the Neutrality of all creations, and the truth that all creations are resources tailored to suit your needs, you will live in a continual state of discomfort. However, you will find balance if you can recognize that you are a Conscious Creator that has unlimited resources available to choose from. If you can accept that resources will come to you as needed and depart when it is time for new growth and expansion, you will find true peace and live your Heaven on Earth. That is all for now. We will recommence in the next lesson, delving further into the Neutrality of all creations and how to vibrationally align your Self with what you desire to have in your life.

LESSON 23
PRACTICING NEUTRALITY

There is so very much to understand in regards to creating your Heaven on Earth; there is so very much, yet there is so very little to it. The main "problem" you have – if we shall call it that – is your resistance, but even this is not really a "problem." Keep in mind throughout this upgrading process that you have dominant data that is going to conflict with what we are teaching you. You are going to have limiting programming that causes resistance to what we are saying. Do not fight this resistance, as to do so would be to push against and actually attract more resistance. Simply align Self through the acknowledgment of your power, be in allowance of the process, and be easy on your Self. Do not condemn the mind for not understanding; instead, be patient with Self, and recognize that this data is currently being perceived as the foreign data or as the data that does not belong. As we continuously expand your knowledge and incorporate new data into the collective of your mind, you will find that the understandings flow more easily and freely. So please, during this process, be easy on your Self, dearest friend. This is all part of the journey. Resistance and then resistance to the resistance, will only yield more resistance. Accept What Is as what has been attracted and what must be to show you the way.

Now, allow us to continue with this most important lesson!

Today, we are going to continue our discussion on the Neutrality of all creations and again give you valuable data to expand your consciousness. As we have stated in the previous lesson, all creations exist on "equal" levels. All creations are neither good nor bad, neither better nor worse. All creations are neutral, and they do not take sides based on Duality. This concept of Duality is what we would like to expand upon today.

To fully comprehend Duality, it is essential that we return to the beginning. As we have indicated, Duality is nothing more than a necessary illusion so that an authentic experience of overcoming the darkness could be presented. In this respect, one could say that Duality really is the core and primary creation necessary for the whole physical experience. But where does Duality begin? Wherein lies the foundation of it all? We believe it is most essential, especially for an analytical mind such as yours, that we always return to the beginning. For achieving an understanding of the origin allows all that was built upon it to fall away that much easier. By understanding the origin of what has frightened you, you will truly understand that there is nothing to fear.

And so we must ponder: what is the origin of this concept of Duality? Well, we know primarily it was intention. The collective intention of nonphysical beings to live a life of physical existence where they would experience the wonderful test of being presented with the darkness, to then ultimately overcome it. All right, and then what? Well, from that point, an authentic testing ground needed to be created. A world were one could truly immerse themselves in the illusion of it all. A world where one could forget who they truly were, so that the real test would be remembering their true nature! Now, as we have learned previously, with this illusion of Self disassociation sprang the creation of the Ego Self – but in reality, this of course was always the plan! Let us reflect upon this Ego Self for a moment. It is the side of you that reflects the darkness, the side in opposition and the side that represents the Dueling counterpart to Higher Self. And it is here that we find the true origin to all that is perceived with a Duality based mindset. Indeed, it was with the creation of the dueling mind that man came to perceive the possibility of darkness at all. It was with the launching of the Ego Self that man noticed dueling opposites and struggle. What primarily existed as a world with choice became a world with an option of lack. A world were lack was perceivable and tangible and frightening to a disconnected Self. One may wonder what it was that came first – the disconnect or the perception of lack? But in reality, both occurred instantaneously, for a thought of lack could not have occurred while in Authentic Self Alignment.

As the darkness began to incorporate into one's life, as ALL truly began to feel Duality through the created Ego Self counterpart, incarnated beings began incorporating this internal battle between "good" and "evil" into all of their physical experiences. People began to label all that they perceived with this Duality based mindset. They created oppositions and struggle – identifying one creation as being good and another as bad. When in reality, all possible creations were simply neutral resources to assist, and although the veil of Duality had shrouded man's eyes, it was always simply a matter of choice. Once the option of lack entered the mind and separation was perceived, there was a continual descent into the darkness of the unseen. Man no longer perceived the Truths of his reality or the nature of his power, and he fully immersed himself in the illusion of it all.

However, as dark as it may seem – there has always been the light; always the way home. Always the voice inside that brought hope and peace. The voice that guided and truly orchestrated, ensuring that all was not lost. Through the ages, that voice was often silenced by choice so that the Earth could undergo her own cleansings and rapid periods of growth. Nevertheless, that voice of the true one that dwells within has never departed humanity. And so the time has finally come that the world collectively finds itself ready for a drastic change. A time where humanity is now, ready to live the alternative side of the coin.

We have waited eons living past lives of a suppressed nature, ensuring that all followed the plan as was intended. However, in this life, we can fully emerge as who we are. We can come forward as the great Masters that we are, without fear and without hesitation. In the past, we remained silent in the shadows – immersed in a world that was not ready for the Truth. But with each passing age, the collective has grown and expanded and witnessed the veil of Duality disintegrating before their eyes! Now is the time for all to see the Truth of who they are! Now is the time for all to perceive the beautiful reality of your Duality based world. All will come to see that there is only choice, and although lack is an option – it is not the required choice. As your strength grows and as you collect more and more data supporting your ability to Consciously Create, you will become a mighty advocate in this great plan of revealing.

What a Joyous time to be alive and in physical form. What a Joyous time to be of service!

Now that the origin is truly understood. Now that you truly embrace the parallel between your own Duality within, you can fully comprehend how that which brews in the mind has been conjured and reflected into your own physical experiences. Remove the mindset of Duality and a perceived struggle between light and dark within – and you will remove all outward traces of Duality. As the struggle ceases to exist within your mind, your physical resources will reflect this thinking into experiences of true happiness, peace and balance. You will exist as one, as your beautiful Authentic Self, and you will reap rewards far greater than anything you can ever imagine. Embrace who you are and accept every beautiful part of you. For it is all beautiful and it is all necessary – it is all an essential part of the plan!

Allow us now to continue with your perception of Duality on the physical plane. Let us discuss how many of you are still perceiving the creation process, and let us once and for all dissolve the illusion of Duality!

In your society, you view everything in your existence as having an opposite. There is hot and there is cold; there is light and there is dark; there is wealth and there is poverty, so on and so on. Such is a necessity for the perception of a Dualistic world of opposites in opposition. Although we do not deny the obvious opposites of things such as "hot and cold", what we are referring to goes much deeper than the superficial correlations made in this statement. Your society operates on this notion of good and bad dualities for the mere purpose of growth and expansion, i.e. without the darkness, one cannot notice the light. This is an essential part of your path, but what we are attempting to express today is the level of consciousness that must be achieved in order for you to reach a point of Non-Duality or as we prefer – Neutrality. Why is Neutrality essential? Simply because Duality exists at a level of consciousness that provides the opportunity to take note of the "differences" that exist within all of your creations. The differences between the opposite creations that you label with a Dualistic mindset as your "good" and "bad" creations, on both an individual and global scale. This dual concept thinking was essential to equip you with necessary data and prepare you for the next stage. You not only needed to experience Duality on a personal level, you needed to sense this perceived struggle between good and bad on a global scale so that you could understand the role you were to play. Although Duality is often perceived as an unwanted part of existence, the time immersed within Duality based consciousness was essential to your path. For you could not understand what you wanted to stand up for, if you did not perceive the difference. Once this level of consciousness is understood and mastered, it is then essential to move forward. With this expansion comes the acceptance that in reality there are no sides: all is One! But the fact still remains that your choices for your desired path in this physical life would not have come to be without an immersion in the Duality consciousness and a taste of the difference between the perceived sides!

From this great leap of expansion comes the age of the Conscious Creator. From this consciousness, you now understand that in order to attract all that you desire, you must have your attention on that which you desire at all times. In order for you to maintain attention to that which you desire, you must come to see all creations for what they truly are. You must come to see that all creations are essentially the same and only vary in degrees. Now let us expand on what we mean by this.

As a Conscious Creator, if you were to continue to see the light and dark of everything and you were to continue to perceive unwanted creations, you would only proceed to create Attachments to that which you say you no longer desire. Why is this? This occurs simply because of the Attachment created by the concept of a "bad" creation and a "good" creation. A bad creation implies something that is unwanted and will make you unhappy, whereas a good creation implies something that is wanted and will, as a result, make you happy. From this mindset, you become dependent on the good creation for happiness, and you fear the bad creation out of concern for this same state of happiness. However, when you view creations from a neutral standpoint of Neutrality, you see that there are no good or bad creations and that all creations are simply neutral and varying degrees of one another. You realize that this determination of good or bad is simply Duality based thinking and a mere reflection of your individual perspectives! You come to the understanding that all creations in the physical stem from ONE vibration – Source Energy – and it is this ONE vibration that is "distorted," which then turns the "best" possible version of a creation into the "worst" possible version, or really any degree in between, based on your Dualistic thinking and limiting beliefs. If you cease your Dualistic thinking and you achieve a state of Neutrality in all creations, you will do away with this concept. You will come to see that all creations are equal and of the same basic vibration. You will see that it is only you that distorts the optimal creation into this good or bad category, by focusing on what you say you do not want and directing Universal Source Energy into the creation that you CHOOSE. In reality, all is simply choice. One's Dualistic mindset produces limitations to the creation that are not at all necessary and can be removed with choice!

For the purpose of examination, let us continue to use this opposite state of "Hot and Cold" expressed earlier to further your understandings. We use these obvious opposites to better explain the varying degrees of creations available to you and to express the true nature of all creation. For this example, let us specifically discuss the varying possible temperatures of water. When raising and lowering the temperature of water, the water itself remains the same whether it is hot or cold. It does not cease to be water, simply because it is hot, and it does not cease to be water simply because it is cold. It is always water, and yet you create the varying degree that determines which way the water tends toward. You determine which degree you will choose. The same logic can be applied to your creations. Regardless of how you direct Source Energy and despite which degree of the Ultimate Source vibration you choose, every creation you produce will still be the same Source Energy. All creations, regardless of how they are perceived with a Dualistic mindset, are of the same Source Vibration, and ALL are of the light. To place blame or false judgment upon a creation is to inadvertently cast shame upon the Source, as Source IS the life force of All That IS.

To further expand upon this example, let us now discuss your perception of the opposites – Hot and Cold. What is labeled as Cold and what is labeled as Hot is subjective and determined based on individual perspectives. When you analyze basic water temperatures, you would not logically say that either opposite is Bad or Good, you would simply say that each opposite provides a resource when needed; you would say that these are neutral resources. It would seem illogical from this neutral perspective to cast such opposites into a role of Duality; yet it is done all the time, when one, for example, burns their mouth or receives a painful toothache from a cold beverage. Due to a Duality based mindset, humans are capable of casting any opposite creation into the role of opposites in opposition simply because it is their nature to do so. But in reality neither creation is good nor bad, both are simply a possible option to choose from. But while immersed in the illusion of Duality, the mind easily takes the neutral opposites and creates opposition. It is at this moment that one forgets choice and attraction and simply blames their creation – deflecting from their own accountability. While immersed in the illusion of what is perceived as unwanted, you fail to remember your role in attracting what you do not want. Instead of simply analyzing the data that led to the physical manifestation of the opposite and proceeding to make a new choice, one simply blames exterior sources and fears the neutral resource, thus preventing the opportunity to learn from what was attracted and create something new!

Furthermore, when analyzing this concept of Hot and Cold, we can also conclude the illogical nature of labeling with extreme opposites. There is not simply Hot and Cold – there exists numerous varying degrees of temperatures, as evident by the varying numbers on a thermometer. One does not simply have to choose Hot or Cold. They have various other options to choose from if they are not satisfied with what they experience from the extreme opposites. They are presented with a vast array of water temperatures they can create simply with choice! What temperature one chooses is not difficult to create, it is simply a different method for the degree desired.

Why choose this concept of water temperatures? Well, simply because it is a seemingly meaningless neutral creation, which most would simply say is not relevant to other pertinent opposite creations such as: Wealth and Poverty, Health and Disease, Abundance and Lack. It would appear this way, but in reality this concept of Hot and Cold water is entirely the same. ALL opposites are merely the absence of one another. Such is the purpose of Duality – to truly perceive tangible extremes and further the illusion of a world of possible opposites. A world of choice! Regardless of what opposite you choose, they are essentially one and the same and represent varying degrees of one another. In every single case, despite how neutral the resource may appear initially, humans are capable of taking this neutral resource and presenting a Dualistic mindset to it – labeling one side "Good" and the other side "Bad." But what humans fail to see is that their Attachment created from the labeling of their creations is what prevents them from focusing on the desired alternative! We can apply this same concept to all of your creations. You are not merely presented with two choices – with a good or bad choice. You are presented with unlimited choices that represent a vast array of varying degrees of extreme opposites. Simply because these obvious opposites exist to provide an authentic array of choices does not mean that either creation must favor Duality. All creations and their varying degrees simply provide choice and option!

So what we propose in all of your creative endeavors is that you look at the choosing of creations/resources much the same way as you would choose the temperature of your water. You should not look at your desire for something and say, "It is much more difficult to create the abundant version of this creation, than it is to create the less abundant version." This concept is as illogical as saying, "It is much more difficult to bring this water to a cold temperature, than it is to bring this water to a hot temperature." It is not more difficult to do either, given your vast resources to do so. It is simply a different process for both. When you examine your creations, do not view it as being more difficult to shift to another version of your creation, look at it as simply utilizing a different method. Your creations all exist as possible options, as does the varying potential water temperatures. They are all neutral and all easily attainable; it is simply choice that determines what you will produce. Having great abundance is no different than having little abundance, except for the varying degrees between them; but fundamentally, they are the exact same Source Energy and only appear different on a superficial level, based on the chosen mental method of creation.

Now let us move onto the practical aspect of this lesson. We are going to turn your attention once again to the previously discussed: Two Methods of Creation. What we have examined thus far has told you that you have two options. You can either choose to Maintain a creation that is desired, or you can choose to Transmute & Initiate. In regards to the method of Maintain, it should be obvious when this option is a relevant method for your creative endeavors. There are many things in your experiences that you desire to keep in your experiences, such as a loved one, house, current financial state, your pets, etc. In this case, your dominant method for these creations is to Maintain their existence in your experiences. Now, that does not mean that these creations cannot be fine-tuned to allow you to experience even more Joy; in fact, we encourage you to improve all aspects of your life, and we will explain this in greater detail later. In these moments when you are pleased with what you have created and you do not want to transmute, you need only choose to maintain what you currently have attracted. All resources are maintained as easily as they are created – by your desire that it be so.

Let us move onto the Second Method of Creation: Transmute & Initiate. In respect to this Method of Creation, this is the process by which you choose to produce a different vibrational frequency or a different degree of your creation. However, in order for you to choose a new degree of your creation, you must first recognize the current degree that you are attracting. This is achieved by utilizing the vast knowledge that you have been presented with in these lessons. Allow your Self to practice your understandings of the Four Core Limiting Beliefs and the Three Steps of Realization so that you may do away with any limiting beliefs that are preventing transmutation. Maintain the understanding that all creations are neutral – one is not better or harder to achieve then another – and release your Attachment to the creations that are preventing you from allowing a proper transmutation of that which you say you do not want. Last is the fun part, the visualizations, which will Initiate the manifestation of your desire on the physical plane!

As you become more and more versed in this process of eliminating Attachment by automatically addressing the responsible Core Limiting Belief and immediately acknowledging the Neutrality of all creations – you will find your Self able to create that much easier. Although it is really only necessary for you to focus on a desired creation once, visualizations are a wonderful tool in allowing your Self to come into vibrational alignment with the degree of the resource you desire. As indicated in a previous lesson, when you experience past data surfacing which you have already Recognized, Analyzed and committed to Re-Strategize, we suggest that you utilize the Scale Visualization, discussed in Lesson 18. This will allow your Self to re-engage Authentic Self Alignment and further the reprogramming process. Although this is a most important visualization to remember, today, we are going to expand upon your visualization knowledge. Now that the transmutation process is fully understood, we are going to begin discuss a new process of visualization, geared toward allowing you to Initiate your desired creation on the physical plane.

Visualizations are yet another tool that has been misinterpreted by the masses. So many have used visualizations without understanding exactly how and why visualizations can be of great service to you. Many perceive this concept of "imagery creation" as a fail proof method for bringing that which one desires into their lives. However, they have forgotten that a visualization without the proper programing to support it, is useless in the Reality Creation Process. We do not imply that a visualization cannot still assist one in achieving a desired state of Authentic Self Alignment, through the brief Joy experienced.

What we are saying is that visualizations alone are not beneficial in the creation process. What has been discussed in this manual is necessary reprogramming, which is essential to ensure that the creation is allowed by the mind and initiated on the physical plane. So many utilize visualizations, thinking that they will magically solve all of their problems and they ignore the reprogramming that is essential to the process of a successful visualization. They do not see that a visualization practiced without a mind free of distorting limiting beliefs will yield undesirable results. They think that by simply performing a few visualizations they will undo the effects of all of their thoughts produced by limiting beliefs. You, however, have come to understand many great Truths that will assist you in achieving optimal results from your visualizations!

To begin, let us first discuss the purpose of visualizations. Visualizations are images created by the physical brain that allows the mind to "try out" a desired experience. If a visualization is successful, the vibrations presented in said visualization will then Initiate the desired creation on the physical plane. The process of Visualization can likewise be used in a detrimental manner, in the sense of using this wonderful powerful tool to create so called "unwanted" experiences. But remember, as we have said, your attention to it signifies your desire of it. So really there are no unwanted experiences. What we will focus your attention on in these lessons is the desired experiences. So, what exactly occurs during a visualization that is deemed a success? Well, during this process, the physical brain creates images based on collected data. The brain strings together a series of images based on what you desire to see.

You can so very easily direct the brain to project precisely what you desire to see, but you must learn to master your thoughts to do so. When an image is projected on the "mental screen," it will then invoke an "emotion." It is this emotion that indicates the creations alignment with the intentions of Self. The better the feeling, or the happier the emotion, the more in tune it is with your inner knowing. If the feeling leans toward a sense of negativity, you are receiving a signal form your Emotional Indicator that you are not in tune with the intentions of Self.

Now, let us examine the process of an ideal visualization. When performing this process, it is important to remember that projection is not necessary nor recommended. As previously discussed, projection of a "better" experience into the desired future is often laced with fearful Duality based thinking. You do not need to set the intention to create a future that is superior to what you have now, you simply are to set the intention for what you choose to experience next, doing so with no Attachment to what you currently have and what you desire to have. It is simply a choice – not a means of escape. When you perform your visualizations, command the mind to bring forward ALL data that is relevant to your desire for Joy. By focusing on this "feeling" of Joy, the mind upon your command will instantly bring forward all previously collected data that vibrationally matched this feeling. These impressions could present as a vast array of resources that you have come across that triggered desire within you. When you allow images of desired creations to flood your mind's eye from previously received data, your physical brain is operating at its most useful capacity. It is providing you with images from data that match the intention of your desired feeling.

In this sense, the Joyous feeling you desire is NOT dependent on your creations; rather your creations summoned are dependent on the Joyous feeling, thus preventing Attachment. From this perspective, you are viewing your potential creations from a mindset of Neutrality and you are simply choosing the creation that optimally serves you! The key to successful visualization is to optimally utilize the mind and physical brain as the tools they are meant to be used as. Draw upon the vast knowledge of the mind, and command it to bring forth data relevant to your current intention of seeking Joy. Control it, and do not allow it to control you. Set the intention to create experiences filled with pure Joy and allow the mind to conjure up all data that has been collected, which triggered and signaled Joy on your Emotional Indicator. Allow the mind to provide you with the desired creations that match your intention for Joy, and do not allow the creations to dictate your level of Joy allowed, based on limiting beliefs. REMEMBER, all creations are neutral; they are simply resources for your Joy, and you should have no Attachment to them. As a Conscious Creator, your Joy is not determined by your creations, rather your creations are determined by your Joy! Ponder what we have discussed and practice, practice, practice! We will begin the next lesson with a period of review and reflection, followed by a supplementary discussion on visualizations!

LESSON 24
REVIEW & REFLECTION

In this lesson, we will continue sharing our most valuable perspectives on Conscious Reality Creation. To begin, we would like to take some time to review and reflect upon a few limiting beliefs that plague the majority at this stage of Self Expansion. We will take this time to examine these concepts so that we may ensure that you are ready to move forward in your creative endeavors.

Firstly, we wish to discuss this commonly experienced stage where you become convinced that you are incapable of releasing that which you no longer desire to experience. We will stress yet again, that your Fear of Failure has resulted in you inventing an Attachment to your creations. You are not viewing creations as Neutral and instead you are deeming one "worse" and one "better," and as a result, this Dualistic mindset has created an Attachment to your creations, i.e., "Well, I most certainly do not want this worse creation; I want the better creation, but I am living within this worse creation, and I can't just avoid how miserable it makes me." Or, "I strongly desire this better creation, but what if I am stuck forever with the bad creation, and what if I do not achieve the creation I want so desperately?" These are examples of the many thoughts that are produced as a result of your Attachment to a Duality based mindset and ultimately your Attachment to your creations. Your Duality based mindset has created a mental struggle between what has currently been attracted and what is desired. As a result, you have produced an Attachment and a continual mental struggle between focusing on the "bad" and focusing on the "good" simply because you are fearful of the bad. All thoughts related to either opposite stems from a completely fear based Dualistic mindset and will certainly not match the vibrational frequency of the abundance you say you desire. Seeing as all thoughts contribute to your creations, these thoughts then determine what you will allow in your experiences. Your attention to that which you no longer desire keeps you tied to that which you no longer desire. You must come to an understanding that all creations are Neutral and that ALL creations do not sway in either direction, to favor the concept of "good or bad." All resources are merely varying degrees of the same Source vibration, and ALL are on the same level of Neutrality.

To expand upon this, let us now address the next limiting belief associated with the Reality Creation Process. Many of you still cling to your low Self-Worth issues, and as a result, you believe that you do not deserve particular creations. What we would like to emphasize is how this Self-Worth Core Limiting Belief very closely relates to your lack of acceptance of Neutrality and ultimately creates great discomfort during the creation process. You see, you are perceiving one creation as being superior to another, and as a result, you are creating Attachments to your creations. Now combine this with your low Self-Worth, which makes you think that you do not deserve anything "better," and you have created quite the vibrational block preventing that which you say you desire. As we have stated before, your Self-Worth issues are nothing but the manifested result of your discomfort from Authentic Self misalignment. Your displacement that began on the mental plane, manifested in various ways on the physical plane as you feeling out of place, different, unworthy, unimportant, incompetent, etc. These physical situations then resulted in your low Self-Worth; but remember, these physical plane manifestations ALL began on the mental plane. They came forth as a result of your discomfort within Ego Self connection and your strong desire to re-engage Authentic Self Alignment and fulfill your Global Purpose. From the moment you entered the physical plane, this path was always your destiny, and so there are multiple things to consider here. All of your Self-Worth "offshoot" limiting beliefs merely stem from your discomfort with a disengaged Authentic Self, which manifested onto the physical plane as situations resulting in this sense of low Self-Worth. In reality, there is no reason for you to feel low Self-Worth as you are a Divine Creator, whose birthright is to have whatever reality is desired! You are a physical incarnation of the infinite Source Energy, and you are destined to have whatever it is you desire, but in order to achieve this, you MUST remember the Neutrality of all creations. One creation is not "better" than the other. There is no Duality. There are only Neutral creations – ample choices – all of which are available for the taking. It is simply a matter of choice.

Let us now shift our attention to the limiting belief that affects so many of you during the Reality Creation Process: TIME.

So many of you have difficulty maintaining your vibration while you wait for your creation to manifest on the physical plane. You are beings who are used to instantaneous results in your pure vibrational state, and so the waiting period can be difficult for you. This limiting belief is most closely associated with the Self-Worth and Fear of Failure Core Limiting Beliefs. Allow us to explain further. In the sense of this "time" concept, the primary concern is that as you wait for your creation to manifest onto the physical plane, you begin to doubt your ability to create altogether. As you see the days pass and you see no results, the data in your mind proceeds to tell you that you have been misinformed about your power to create. The mind then provides you with ample data related to unsuccessful creative endeavors, as proof that you have been wrong many times in the past. If you do not remain firm in your understandings of the function of the mind, you can proceed into a panicked state believing that this could yet again mean failure. Well, let us provide you with a few new perspectives on this matter.

Firstly, we need to address the thoughts that enter your mind in the above situation. These thoughts are merely past data; data-thoughts that the mind is bringing forward to assist you. The mind is an amazing tool filled with copious amounts of data, but because deliberate Reality Creation is new to you, you will have limited data based on success. Therefore, in every moment that you allow in data, the mind will simultaneously provide relevant information to assist you in your current experience. Remember that the mind is your tool! The mind exists to serve you, and the mind is only providing data to contribute relevant information to your current experience so that you may make an informed decision. Simply because the majority of data that you have on Conscious Reality Creation states that you have not succeeded in the past, this does not mean that you must give in to this past programming. In these moments, you are presented with an opportunity to reprogram the mind, but you must do so by providing new data to run a seamless Conscious Reality Creator program. You need only smile and recognize the beautiful task that your mind is performing. You must have gratitude for the hard work of your beautiful mind and its ability to provide you with relevant data to assist you in making an informed decision. You must not be angry or spiteful at your mind, as it is performing its function with perfection. You must realize that to hate your mind is to hate your Self. So friend, let us remind you that these data-thoughts that enter your mind are attempting to assist you. If they do not provide information that is relevant to your new intention, simply let them pass, and do NOT misinterpret the data. Do NOT mistake the data for confirmation that you have failed, consequently allowing your Self to call upon your Core Limiting Beliefs. Once you are able to accomplish this, you will have successfully transmuted that which no longer serves you.

Secondly, it is important that we explain what is really meant by this waiting period in the Reality Creation Process. So many of you perceive a waiting period, or a period of time passing, between your asking and your receiving. But again, your senses have only revealed a partial Truth. There is no specific waiting period and no designated amount of time for your creations to manifest on the physical plane. There is simply a Period of Clarity. It is the perceived "time" that is taken for you to collect the necessary data to produce the optimal vibrational frequency of what is desired. There is no set time because, in reality, time has nothing to do with it. It is simply a Period of Clarity. Once you have received the necessary data to cease resistance and ultimately transmute the vibrational frequency you are offering, you will then Initiate your new desired creation on the physical plane.

So you see, there is no need to be concerned about the passing of time. For time is simply an indicator of moving forward in growth and expansion. These periods between Intention and physical manifestation offer a necessary stage of Self growth, which is unavoidable. In reality, you would never want to avoid the Period of Clarity, or perceived waiting period, for it is in these moments that you prepare your Self to allow that which you desire. The elimination of these periods of Self growth would most certainly ensure that you never receive your desired creation. So know this: The Period of Clarity is not to be feared and approached impatiently. It is essential and required to allow you to receive the optimal resource! Embrace your Periods of Clarity with dedication, eagerness and excitement, accepting that this period will pass, and know that because of your patience and commitment – you WILL see your creation manifested in physical form!

We will conclude this lesson with a final discussion on limiting beliefs associated with the visualization process. As we have indicated in the previous lesson, we believe many of you have approached this visualization process backward. You have determined that your Joy is dependent on your creations, and as a result, you have attempted to force visualizations of what you think you "should" have. What we have proposed is that you realize the Truth; your Joy is not dependent on your creations, but rather your creations must be dependent on your Joy! Allow us to explain further.

More often than not, when you proceed with a specific visualization – imagining your perfect car, your perfect house or your perfect partner – you create visualizations based on what you are used to allowing for Self. These visualizations are often based on limitations that are presented to Self by the limiting beliefs you hold. Now, if you switch your focus from your creations to a focus solely on the emotion of Joy, you will find much greater success. Many of you perform your visualizations and wonder why your mind begins to wonder, or your fears are allowed to interrupt the process. Well, simply put, it is because the visualizations do not hold you or captivate you, and this is because they do not have the emotion required to keep your attention. If you are to switch your intention for your visualizations, from focusing on the creations and instead focusing on the emotion of Joy, you will find amazing results. We suggest that you begin your visualizations by commanding the mind to display data relevant to the desired emotion of optimal Joy! Allow your mind to bring forth visualizations of your deepest and most Joyous desires, based on previously collected Joy-based data. Have fun with this, and do not allow your past programming to creep in and tell you that these things are not possible; simply allow your Self to be fully engaged in the visualization process.

Allow us to further expand upon this visualization process, to provide tools that will assist you. We suggest that as you walk through your day, you allow your Self to fully feel the energy associated with every experience you have, including every object that you come in contact with. Simply focus on your surroundings with a quiet mind. Allow your Self to completely embrace What Is. Move from one object/experience to the next and simply note how what you are perceiving makes you feel. The energy you "Feel" will then be interpreted by your Emotional Indicator, and you will be able to determine how this resource would serve you. Do not over analyze, simply learn to listen to what your Emotional Indicator is telling you, based on the energy your body is detecting. Become hypersensitive to all that exists around you – the people, the animals, the objects. Learn to connect with them using all of your senses – including your sense of Feeling! Not only will this allow you to remain as a Conscious Creator at all times, this will also allow your mind to collect the data that you require for your visualizations.

As you walk through your day, fully allow your Self to embrace EVERY experience. Feel the Joy that is sensed from resources you have perceived that you would like to experience in your life and likewise do so for resources that you are currently attracting within your life. You can collect the new data of what is desired from all sorts of sources: another person, the media, a book or even a catalog! While you partake in this experience, also allow your Self to feel the emotion that emanates from that which you do not desire to experience. Do not be afraid of this exercise, as you are not asked to take on the emotional vibration perceived by that which you do not desire to experience. This exercise is simply to allow the mind ample data to create a "database" for your visualizations. When you experience something that is not desired, you should simply take note of what your sense of feeling is indicating and move on to search for that which you wish to experience.

You are not asked to dwell on what you feel, you are simply doing this exercise so that you can recognize what you are capable of Feeling. Therefore, allowing your Self to be able to determine the emotion associated with all objects and experiences. As you do this more often, you will begin to feel the varying degrees of vibration of each object and experiences. You will begin to feel, through your built-in energy receptors, how you resonate with each and every experience and object. You will begin to notice possibilities that feel great and possibilities that do not. You will begin to feel possibilities that trigger happiness and more importantly, you will begin to feel possibilities that bring you complete and utter Joy.

Now, you may be wondering, "Is this not determining that one creation is better than the other, by searching for a better emotion?" Allow us to explain. You are not rating the creation; you are using your sense of Feeling to determine the produced emotion. You are not saying that one creation is better than the other, you are simply deciding which Neutral resource will best assist you on your path. From this perspective, there is absolutely no Attachment to the resources, and your goal is simply to determine and focus upon that which brings you Joy! Your resonance with the creation really has nothing to do with the actual vibration of the experience or object, but rather, it has everything to do with the creations or objects ability to assist you in your growth and expansion. Therefore, it is not a ranking of the creation but rather a determination of how this resource can assist you moving forward.

When you receive this Feeling of Joy, where is it that this Feeling is coming from? Is it not coming from Authentic Self

Alignment? Yes, it is an indication that this creation is desired, by Self, for personal growth and expansion as a Conscious Creator, and it is an indication that this creation serves you well. When you come across a creation that does not bring about Joy and instead feels of a "Joyless emotion," this is an indication that Self has no desire to experience this object or situation. As in most cases, Self has already received ample data from resources such as these. It is important to remember what the goal of Conscious Reality Creation is: it is to seek out the vibrations of the resources that will optimally assist you on your path. What you must focus upon is how the neutral experience/resource Feels, to determine how it rates on your Emotional Indicator or Joy scale. You are to determine if the object or experience you have come in contact with, rates high or low on your Emotional Indicator. If it rates low that does NOT mean it is a "bad" resource, it simply means that the data is not desired by Self and similar data has most likely already been collected. When following the strategy of searching for the optimal resource, the mind may proceed to then produce this concept of the "worst" option, but in this case you do not need to focus on a Duality based concept. You must thank the mind for the relevant data and put all of our focus on Neutrality.

Focus your attention on your understanding that all resources offer a choice. All resources are available for the taking and one is not harder to achieve than the other – unless one believes it to be so! Focus only on that which is desired and remember the Truths: all creations experienced are truly desired, all creations are wanted for growth and expansion. Duality is an illusion created for the physical world experience, and it is an illusion that you so very easily see beyond. So, when following your Joy scale, search for the optimal resource for your current experience. Always keep in mind that the creations perceived as inferior are NOT inferior at all. Know that at one point in time these creations where the optimal resource for your growth and expansion, whether you consciously realized it or not.

So while performing this exercise, your job is to simply collect data to use in your visualizations. In doing this exercise, you will determine what creations bring you Joy. You will NOT search for creations that produce "so-so" emotions because they are only based on what you think you deserve or what you think you can have. The creations we ask that you seek will provide the optimal emotion, and it is this emotion that will then Transmute your current vibration and Initiate new desired creations.

In the next lesson, we will discuss the concept of Positive Affirmations and explain why they are essential to the Reality Creation Process. We will provide new data on the purpose of affirmations and teach you how to create your own! Excellent work!

LESSON 25
AFFIRMATIONS

What is an affirmation? An affirmation is a set of words that are repeated on a daily bases to produce a vibrational shift in your thought patterns. An affirmation is a wonderful tool that can assist you in Authentic Self Alignment and produce a desired vibrational path. We believe that positive affirmations are extremely useful, but again, as with much of your data, they have been misinterpreted. As a result, many find themselves frustrated with the effects, due to the limiting beliefs they have created out of this affirmation process. Affirmations can be a most marvelous tool when used correctly. They are able to direct and focus your attention on that which you desire to achieve, and they are capable of shifting your energetic point of attraction instantaneously. Affirmations, however, despite popular belief, are not magical words that will ensure you have what you desire. Many approach affirmations believing that reciting a few simple words will then solve all problems caused by insufficient programming. Let us explain again, you operate the way you do simply because of your programming. The mind runs the program of Self that has been downloaded via Higher Self, and if the new necessary data has not been integrated, you will find poor results in the affirmation process – regardless of how many affirmations you recite. Affirmations become a powerful tool when it is understood how thoughts create reality. They become an excellent ally in the creation process, only when it is understood that reprogramming must occur in order to balance out the outdated limiting data that is preventing the Initiation of your desired creation. So please remember, affirmations are not a quick fix. You cannot expect to simply say a few words and then find your Self with your desired results when you continue to think and operate the way you do. This defies law. You must learn mental discipline and control in order to find any real results from affirmations. Only through obtaining the data required to understand how to master your thoughts will you then be able to maintain the vibration set forth by these affirmations.

Now that we understand what affirmations are not, let us discuss what affirmations can do for you in the Reality Creation Process. As we have stated previously, affirmations shift your vibrational alignment so that you can keep your Self on vibrational track. This does NOT mean that you need to repeat affirmations over and over and over; this simply means that affirmations would benefit you one to two times daily. You are NOT reciting these affirmations in an attempt to brainwash your Self – you are performing these affirmations to direct your point of attraction. For example: by setting your focus on the resources you wish to achieve when you wake in the morning, you have now set the vibrational tone for the day. By placing your desires in your line of sight, from the get go, you know what resources to expect. We do not believe that affirmations should be work. It should a Joyous moment where you focus on the resources that you desire, and it should provoke optimal desires and Joy-based vibrations within you.

We propose that when writing affirmations, you do away with any limiting beliefs you have about what is required for a successful affirmation. This notion is but an offshoot limiting belief of Perfectionism, one of the Four Core Limiting Beliefs. There is no cookie cutter model; there are no precise words that must be said. Many have taught that you must "subliminally trick" the mind with specific words and codes to see any real results. To this we say: it is not necessary. There is no tricking or brainwashing required. With reprogramming, you are quite capable of making these changes in a very conscious and active state. When you choose to write these words they should cause optimal vibrations within you. Do not be concerned with what anyone else thinks of your private affirmations, as they are meant for you. They do not even have to be understood by anyone else. Simply put, they only have to resonate with you and trigger an optimal vibration within you! Remember, it is not the words that do a thing, it is the vibration that is created as a result of the resonance with the data brought forth. Essentially, the words yield data that when strung together to form your affirmation, trigger the perfect concoction of desire! We will offer you our perspectives on what we believe to be the most useful use of affirmations, based on our own experiences, but as always we encourage you to do what feels right for you!

So let us have fun with this. Let us take a load off and find the Joy in this lesson! Let us continue with **Writing Affirmations 101:**

When writing an affirmation, use your sense of Feeling to find the optimal emotional response:

This means, do not write your "so – so" desire or your mediocre version of your desire. This means stating the ultimate desire that would create the ultimate emotion of Joy. Again, do not be concerned with what others think of your dreams. You know the scope of your creative abilities, so why would you limit your Self when you can so easily have your most desired dreams. Remember all creations are Neutral. It is no more difficult to create one object or experience over another. It is simply a choice!

When writing an Affirmation, do not get caught up in the words:

The words, although they may represent the data that triggers the resonance, are really unimportant. A single word is insignificant, but when placed together, they paint a picture or create a concoction for your own personal dose of Joy. Remember to not worry about individual specific words, i.e. if they sound intelligent enough or creative enough. Simply concentrate on how the overall words make you feel. Many who write affirmations get so caught up on whether or not a word sounds right or means precisely what they are intending to say, that they miss the whole point of affirmations and find it to be a miserable experience. There is no need to plague your Self with limiting beliefs based on Perfectionism. There is no one right way to write an affirmation, and there is no one to judge you for your writing skills or your desires. These are just for you. So have fun!

241

When writing an Affirmation, do not discuss specific objects or experiences:

Allow us to explain what we mean by this. During the affirmation writing process, you are to use your sense of Feeling, and you are to write words that trigger an ultimate Joy-based emotion for Self. Because this process is not meant to "specifically" create but merely set a vibrational tone for all creations, it is best to keep the affirmations general and more generic to suit your various desires and life experiences.

For example: I am an abundant person. I allow all aspects of abundance into my life. I am receiving a continual flow of Joyous abundance at every moment of every day. I feel abundant, and my thoughts of abundance reflect greatly in all of my experiences.

Now, in this particular example, we have chosen to focus on Abundance. We have not chosen money specifically, as we are not interested in the specific objects for this exercise. This exercise is to search for the best overall emotion, in relation to ALL that is desired. When you perform your visualizations, this is the perfect time to compile all the data that you have collected that matches this exact Joyous emotion and Initiate creations focused on specific desires. Affirmations are simply to set the vibrational tone for All of your creative endeavors, ensuring that you are a vibrational match to all manners of abundance!

Lastly, writing Affirmations should not feel like a chore:

Affirmations are not meant to be a tedious task; they are meant to convey your desired Joy through words. Affirmations are intended to create the emotion of your optimal desires, and every time they are recited, they should create the perfect vibrational alignment to ALL that you desire. So, if it feels like a chore, then we suggest you take a break and come back when you are more vibrationally attuned to the process.

Now that we have addressed the writing process, let us further delve into some of the concepts discussed. As we have stated, the purpose of the affirmation is to set your vibrational tone to allow your desires, and it is most certainly not to brainwash you. In relation to this concept, let us now delve into why we do not feel it is in your best interest to focus on specific objects or experiences that are desired, when utilizing affirmations.

Throughout your life, there are going to be many, many things that you desire. You are going to change these desires on a daily basis, as is your nature and your purpose as a Creator. In Truth, if you lose desire – you lose the will to exist on the physical plane. Now, if you were to create an affirmation for everything that you desire, you would have quite the long list. What we propose is that you create general affirmations, maybe only two or three that you affirm in the morning and before bed, but also midday if you so desire. These Affirmations will cover the basis of your desires to allow all manner of creations to flow into your existence. Let us state again that we believe your affirmations should include whatever you desire for them to include. So, if there is something that you are so eagerly trying to manifest, feel

243

free to create an affirmation for this resource. But it should be addressed why you feel the need for an affirmation for this specific creation? Do you doubt your ability to create from your intention alone? Is there any form of Attachment to this creation – perhaps a limiting belief? Fear, which has resulted in you thinking that you might not achieve this creation and as a result, led you to think that you need to do extra work? When we suggest Affirmations, it is simply to set the tone at the beginning or ending of the day, and as a result, set the vibrational point of attraction for all your thoughts moving forward. Therefore, bringing you into alignment with ALL of your creations.

Moving forward, we will suggest two Affirmations per day as the optimal amount. Allow us to explain why. We believe that there are two general categories for affirmations that encompass all of your desires: Abundance and Mental Control. When pursing the resources that you require, you are always seeking abundance so that what is desired flows freely and easily into your experience. Abundance implies an overflowing supply of what you require, signifying that there is no concern with not having what you need. This is a very important concept to incorporate into your affirmations. As an abundant person, you will allow the Universe to bring you precisely what you need, whether it be an abundance of money, an abundance of love, an abundance of health, etc.

Our second suggested topic for your affirmations is Mental Control. We feel this topic is essential, as it is your thoughts that direct all aspects of your reality, and so affirming statements that empower you and ensure control over your thought patterns are vital. At this moment, it is important to point out that this affirmation will not cause any thought patterns that need to be addressed by the Three Steps of Realization to just go away. To the contrary. An Affirmation such as this will merely allow you the intention of mental discipline when, and only when, you have acquired the necessary tools to practice said mental discipline. Remember, in any situation, you cannot perform the task required without the necessary tools. Arm your Self with required data and you will achieve complete Mental Control. Now, let us proceed to create some examples of affirmations, which we encourage you to mold and shape into your own preferred version. Remember: **FIND THE OPTIMAL EMOTION VIA YOUR SENSE OF FEELING.**

MENTAL CONTROL: I am a master of time and circumstances. I am a powerful creative being, and I have complete control over my thoughts and beliefs. Through my heightened mental control, I continually choose the experiences that I desire. At all times, I ensure that I maintain an optimal balance in my programming so that I may see my disciplined thoughts reflected onto the physical plane.

ABUNDANCE: I am naturally abundant, and I fully accept that it is my birthright to have abundance in all aspects of my life. I am a Divine Creator, and through choice and intention, I am capable of having optimal abundance in all of my experiences. I allow in ample abundance with every breath I take, and I see evidence of my abundant thoughts reflected in all of my surroundings.

We want you to have fun with this process and enjoy the emotion that is produced from writing your affirmations. There is great Joy that can be felt via this process, but you must allow your Self to embrace it whole heartedly while properly understanding the intention behind it. We will end communication on the subject of affirmations and continue in the next lesson, expanding your understanding of the creation process.

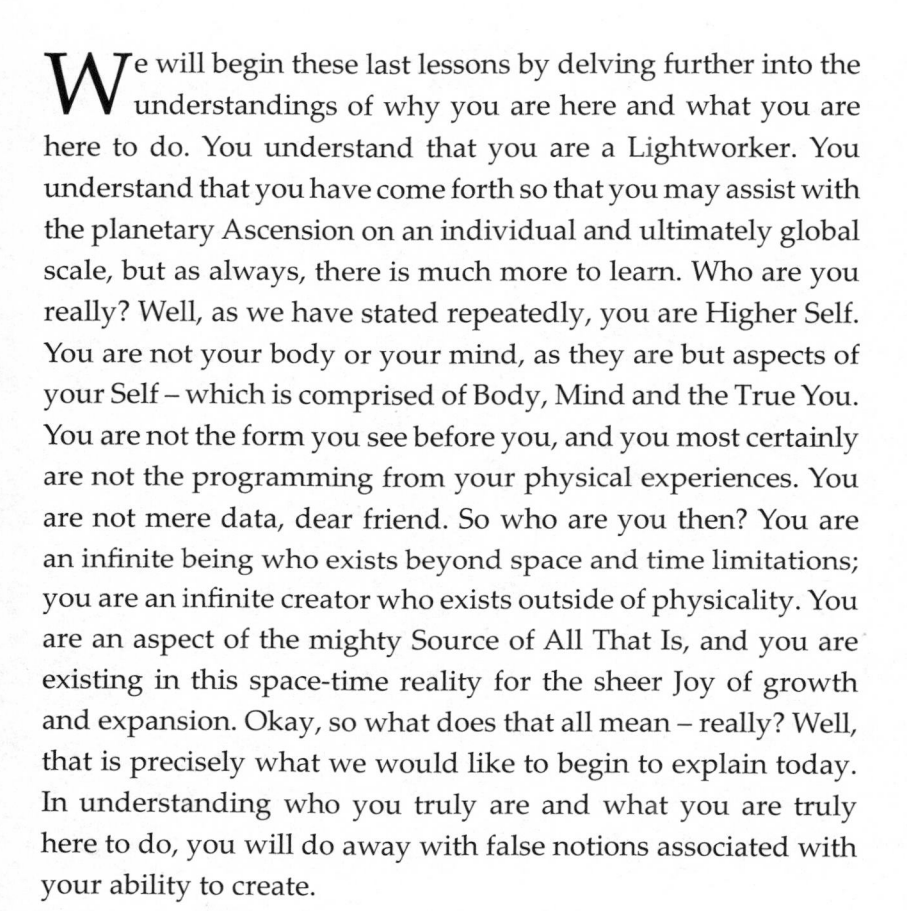

LESSON 26
THE THREE PLANES

We will begin these last lessons by delving further into the understandings of why you are here and what you are here to do. You understand that you are a Lightworker. You understand that you have come forth so that you may assist with the planetary Ascension on an individual and ultimately global scale, but as always, there is much more to learn. Who are you really? Well, as we have stated repeatedly, you are Higher Self. You are not your body or your mind, as they are but aspects of your Self – which is comprised of Body, Mind and the True You. You are not the form you see before you, and you most certainly are not the programming from your physical experiences. You are not mere data, dear friend. So who are you then? You are an infinite being who exists beyond space and time limitations; you are an infinite creator who exists outside of physicality. You are an aspect of the mighty Source of All That Is, and you are existing in this space-time reality for the sheer Joy of growth and expansion. Okay, so what does that all mean – really? Well, that is precisely what we would like to begin to explain today. In understanding who you truly are and what you are truly here to do, you will do away with false notions associated with your ability to create.

What you must first understand is that what you see before you is but one of the three planes. There exists the Physical Plane, upon which all form rests, but there also exists the Mental and Spiritual Planes that are shrouded from your senses. You cannot see them because you have not asked to see them. We will begin by explaining the Three Planes in greater detail.

The Physical Plane – The Physical Plane is dense Energy. At this time, as you currently perceive it with your physical eyes, it exists as a world of shapes and supposed solid structure. You see it as a Three Dimensional model of your reality come to life, but as we have explained previously, this world does not exist as you once believed. There is no dense matter, not really. There are just pieces that come together to create the solid structure you perceive with your senses, but in reality – there is no solid structure at all.

The Mental Plane – The Mental Plane is the plane upon which all data, thought and intention based energy exists. A plane that exists beyond form and as vibration. It is on this plane that all of your desires, your fears, your strengths and your weaknesses pool together to create your individual mind and the Collective Mind for all of mankind. It exists outside of your basic physical senses, but there are many who have expanded their senses to allow themselves to feel this energy. How does one do this you ask? Well, this would be similar to your phrase of "my spidey senses are tingling." It is the use of your sixth sense and the utilization of your built-in "Feeling" sensors that, upon proper activation, allow one to tap into the vibrations that exist all around you at any moment.

The Spiritual Plane – The Spiritual Plane is the plane upon which the True You exists. It is a plane beyond form and thought, and it is a plane that exists as pure energy. It is hard to truly convey what this plane is, as your mind will try to interpret from physical perspectives, and so we will say simply what this plane is not. It is not hot nor cold, neither wet nor dry. It does not have a specific climate like you are used to, and it does not have a specific location. All of these notions are physical world concepts. In reality, this plane simply is as it is. It appears to each as they choose for it to appear, for the spiritual plane exists in perfect harmony with each individual version of Heaven, as will one day come to pass on the physical plane.

When many of you attempt to perceive these planes, you will do so seeing them stacked upon each other, as is your human nature to do so. For you cannot fully comprehend that which exists beyond the physical, as you can only build your interpretation upon limited physical world knowledge. However, your perception of planes stacked upon each other is not the reality of it. These planes exist much so like different substances making up a mixture. In a mixture, the contributing substances perfectly blend and converge to create a flawless concoction, where all individual substances co-exist simultaneously without affecting the composition of one another. If you were not made aware of the individual components of this mixture, you would never recognize the multiple facets of what you were seeing. This is precisely how the planes work. They are there, but to the untrained eye they appear to exist as one.

There is no concern if you are unable to physically see the difference, as your sight is not what is important here. What is essential is your understanding of the concept and your ability to use your sense of "Feeling" to know and operate within all Three Planes. Now, what does this all have to do with creation? Well, in order to achieve success in being a Conscious Creator in all aspects of your life, you must understand how you operate on all Three Planes. You must understand who you truly are in the creation process and do away with any limiting beliefs related to said creation process.

Firstly, you are Self. You are Higher Self experiencing through the physical form known as "Insert your name here." Your mind is the operating system of Self and it runs the "Self Program" based on the combined data that has been collected by Self. Now, what does this have to do with creation? Well, it appears that so many of you do not truly understand your part in creation, since so many of you look at it as though your physical body is responsible for the creation process. You see things that you desire and you believe that the "physical you" has to perform repeated fancy visualizations and that you must recite a million affirmations so that you can convince your Self to receive. Why do you feel the need to do this? We believe it is because you do not fully understand how the creation process works.

Allow us to explain how the process really works. You, Higher Self, desire a new experience on the physical plane. From the spiritual plane, you transmit an intention – via a programming thought that is produced on the mental plane. This new data is then added to the total compilation of Data, in the "Data Bank of Self." This new thought will enter into the mind at the same time as it is being received and recorded in the Collective Mind, as they are in reality one consciousness. This new thought will be something like, "I desire a new house." Now, if the new programming is supported by like data, Self will begin the process of determining the conditions for the desired creation and then ultimately allow the receiving of said new house.

For example:

Self receives a thought indicating a desire for a new house. Self will then proceed to obtain all relevant previously collected data related to the desire for a house. If you have been actively collecting data on houses and determining how said data "Feels" to Self, you will have extensive data to show you what "type" of house Self truly desires to have. Your previously collected data, working as it was intended to, will provide all of the necessary parameters to then allow the visualization of your ideal house to occur, thus, allowing you to Initiate your creation's manifestation on the physical plane. Please note, this is of course an example of an ideal situation. However, for many of you, this is how the process actually goes: The mental plane receives a thought indicating that you, Higher Self, would like to experience a new house. This thought is brought forward and all like data is collected. Along with the data of the ideal house for Self comes related societal data, based on limiting beliefs, i.e. What size of house you should want, so that you are not greedy. How much you can afford, based on the restrictions of your budget and even insecurities about your deserving of a new house.

What we want to attempt to do is reprogram your mind to automatically bypass the unnecessary limiting programming,

251

so that the mind may operate precisely as it was intended to. In order to do this, you must come to a few understandings. You must first and foremost acknowledge that you are Higher Self, and Higher Self is the one desiring the experiences and material items you find in your life. It is not your body or mind that has desired and created them, it is Higher Self. Secondly, you must then come to understand who summons the Universe to form that which is desired; who sets the intention that directs Source Energy. Again, the answer is YOU – Higher Self. The creation does not come from the body or mind, for logic does not suggest that a physical shell and a Self-Operating System could have any creative force. The creative power to summon any and all resources you desire belongs to Higher Self. So, what then is the greatest block in relation to your creative abilities? It is your current belief in who you think YOU are and your current understanding of who is actually creating.

You must remember that it is not the body, for the body is but form and no more than a shell and data collection tool being controlled by YOU. Likewise, it is not the mind. For the mind is merely the operating system of Self and is the manifestation of the Free Will concept; it is simply the way for Higher Self to experience Duality and the solution for Higher Self to have an authentic experience of both the light and dark. No, you are not the mind nor the body. You are Higher Self, and you are the one creating your reality. You have everything figured out. When you are ready for new programming, you send it. When you are ready for a new creation, you send it and you program your avatar to be able to receive it. All creations, whether judged "good" or "bad," were from YOU for YOU and were absolutely necessary for growth and expansion. It is all up to YOU.

There is nothing that is up to the mind or the body, it is all up to you!

For a moment, let us briefly address this concept of the Ego Self because so many of you will once again say, "No, I did not create the things in my life that cause me pain, which I most certainly do not want." To this we say, you most certainly did. You created them for the experiences and data that was necessary to get you to this point. You created them so that you would be faced with the "darkness" and the "bad," and like a phoenix rising from the ashes, you would then pull your Self up and out of adversity to find your way home. You created all of these experiences because you are a Master of time and circumstances. You knew just what situations it would take for you to awaken to the truth. If your life was filled with more sunshine and rainbows and you became content with the mediocrity of un-awakened life, merely believing whatever happens – happens, you would never have made it to this point. No, you needed to see the darkness. You needed to truly see it and feel it so that you would know that this is not the way it has to be for your Self and the world. You had to taste adversity so that you could say, "NO MORE!" and at this point in time, finally allow your Self to overcome your limiting societal programming that has held you in the dark for so long. You programmed every step of the way because you knew it was what was needed to get you to this exact point in time. You knew that without the past you experienced, you would never fulfill your function as an Advocate of Truth.

Why, many will ask, why do this at all? What is the point? Well, for growth and expansion of course, but as always there is something more to be learned. It is in this life that you will achieve growth and expansion like never before. It is in this life that you will put all of your expertise to use and show the world who you ALL truly are. Through your example, it is in this life that you will show the world the Truths and remove the veil from their eyes. You are on Earth, Lightworker, because you are to be an example. You were chosen to be physical because you will proudly and successfully shine the light of truth and, in doing so, show others the way to the new world. Without you, there would be no way. You are the light and an incarnation of the Almighty Source. You are so very important and are an essential part of the plan of All That Is. You will change the world, but first you must begin by recognizing your ability to change your own life. You cannot achieve your goal of assisting the world without first awakening your own flame. For you see, dearest Family, you cannot shine a light for all to see if the light does not already burn brightly within you. That is all for now. We will recommence in the next lesson, furthering your knowledge of the creation process.

LESSON 27
THOUGHTS, CREATION & TIME

For today's lesson, we will continue our discussion on the creation process. We are pleased with your understandings thus far and would like to offer a brief recap of what we have learned together in regards to the creation process. By now, you should understand who "you" are in the creative process. You should acknowledge that you exist as Higher Self and that you are not your body or your mind. You should fully recognize that you are not meant to struggle in the creation process and that it should be a seamless experience of great ease. You should know that creation is a natural ability of yours and fully embrace your capacity to easily and freely partake in the Conscious Reality Creation process. Remember, if you find that you are struggling, it is time to take a step back and reflect on what you have been taught. Today, we would like to begin by furthering your understandings on how the creation process occurs on the Three Planes.

As we have discussed previously, creation always begins on the spiritual plane, moves through the mental plan and then proceeds to manifest on the physical plane. This is always the process for physical existence; there is no exception. As the world that you see before you is merely a physical form representation of your desires and thoughts, it is impossible that any creation could actually stem from the physical plane. The physical plane is but a mirror of the mental plane and ultimately, spiritual plane. Allow us to expand on this further. When we address the actual "path" of a creation, we do so from your perspective of the levels being stacked upon each other. As we indicated before, this is the not the case, but for the physical mind to best understand, we must approach it from this perspective. When a creation is initiated on the spiritual plane via Intention, by the True You – Higher Self, the creation will naturally transition into your experience for manifestation, but first, this creation must direct through the mental plane.

Now, from what you have learned so far, you perceive that it is your thoughts that create the reality you see before you, but even this concept is not entirely accurate. Your thoughts do not create your reality per se, Higher Self does; your thoughts simply act as the filter, which then determines what version of resources you are going to allow. As Higher Self directs Source Energy through Intention, so do your thoughts further direct the same Source energy for manifestation, via the filtering process of the "free will concept." As Higher Self desired an authentic experience of growth and expansion, a test of full immersion in Duality based existence, the mind and its filtering system was the necessary way to provide your infinite Self with an authentic experience of that which was desired. And from this desire sprang forth the manifestation of the mind so that Higher Self could exercise free will and have an authentic experience of darkness – while always reaming safely in one's natural nonphysical state.

Let us use an example to explain how this process of creation works: Higher Self desires a new car. Higher Self, via an intention that produces a thought, makes this desire available to the mind. At this point, the mind has two options: it can allow the optimal version of a car or it can distort the creation of the car by filtering it with limiting beliefs. If the car creation is allowed in its natural state, it will be Self's dream car. If the car is distorted by limiting beliefs, it will be whatever your thoughts have determined you are allowed to have. Once the creation has been launched via Higher Self, acknowledged by the mind and vibrationally attracted by Self, then begins the process of manifestation on the physical plane.

Now understand, the reason that Conscious Reality Creation can become so discouraging to the psyche of an untrained Self is that many modern Reality Creation teachings have led you to believe that the physical aspect of Self – independently – produces creations merely with thoughts. From this perspective, you then spend hours and hours obsessing about what you desire. Believing that through countless affirmations and visualizations that the Universe will bring you what you want because you have been a good little boy or girl and you have done the mental work you were supposed to do. You approach the Reality Creation Process much like an apprentice in the sense that you think you must beg for something from the Universe. When in reality, the universal forces work upon your command, a privilege bestowed upon you as an aspect of the Source Creator. Like so many others, if you feel that you need to do a great deal of work to justify what you desire or feel as though you need to beg permission for something from God, you have been misguided in your learning or have misinterpreted the teachings you have studied. Although some teachings have provided incomplete data regarding the Reality Creation Process, there are many who have spoken Truths on this subject; Truths that if re-examined from a new mindset, will coincide with what we say to you now. You may simply not have understood at the time with your limited perspectives.

As the true creator that you are, as Higher Self, you do not ask for anything – you command it. You do not approach Conscious Reality Creation as something you can accomplish ONLY if you are a good little boy or girl and have completed your Reality Creation chores. In actuality, as a natural Conscious Creator, there is nothing that need be done other than a simple Intention. You do not need to perform numerous routines and recite various thoughts to create what is desired. For if the desire exists, so does the creation, and it is your thoughts that simply direct what version of the creation you allow. But for the majority of those who have not reprogrammed the mind and come to realize these things, they spend countless hours performing these creation chores in an attempt to counteract their limiting data. They fail to see that regardless of the chores they perform, they will never succeed as a Conscious Creator if they attempt to perform creation from a physical perspective alone. The implication that work needs to be done to create blatantly implies that one does not yet understand what aspect of Self is truly creating. To believe that creation is work is to believe in a world of Duality and struggle to obtain what is desired. A Conscious Creator lives beyond this world, understanding that there are no opposites in opposition, no struggle between what is wanted and unwanted that must be fought with countless chores – there is simply choice! There IS only commanding and receiving. There is only choice: **HIGHER SELF'S CHOICE – YOUR CHOICE!**

When you look at the creative process as creations originating from your thoughts and you perceive a "power struggle" that you must win in order to stay aligned with the correct vibrational frequency – you are identifying with the mind. If you embraced that it is you – Higher Self – who chooses all creations, you would look at these perceived moments of struggle and perceived "unfulfilled" creations much differently. You would understand that these moments are because you are still in the "Conscious Creator Program" data collection stage. You would know that you are still obtaining valuable knowledge during these moments; knowledge that will allow you to operate your Conscious Creator Program. What many would perceive as a failure in Conscious Reality Creation is a beautiful success and the completion of a necessary step in the journey of becoming a Conscious Creator. A step that was the choice of Self, for necessary growth and expansion.

Please know, if you have thoughts that prevent you from receiving the optimal creation, which you have set forth from the spiritual plane, this is occurring as it is meant to. It is because you have not received the necessary data to operate the version of Self that can consciously create what is desired. It is because YOU know that you must complete necessary steps and receive necessary reprogramming data in a sequential order to get you to your ultimate goal of returning Self to a powerful Conscious Creator! Stop spending so much time laboring and worrying about not having what you desire and remember who is really in charge. You, Higher Self, are in charge, ALWAYS, and every step of the path is a necessary part to achieving what is desired. If you do not yet have what you long for it is because it is not yet truly desired by Self! You are still expanding and learning from your current experience or else it would not be. And when you have achieved the growth that is desired from your current resources, you will be ready to release them and allow something new. But all must happen in sequential order of the appropriate steps, at the appropriate time, or what is desired will never come to be. You must stop making the path so difficult by offering resistance with body and mind identification. Allow what will be to unfold as it is meant to and, in doing so, find great peace in your experiences.

Now, even in us saying this, please remember that this is all part of your journey! You are meant to identify with the body and mind. As this is the choice of the True You, Higher Self, and is all part of the test and choice of a "Free Will" experience! Self must battle identifying with either the Physical Self or the Spiritual Self until they come to realize they are one and the same! This is all part of the Joyous game. The teachings we offer you today are meant to provide the last bit of programming that is essential so that you can now begin a new version of Self. A version of Self that operates as Self 2.0. An upgraded multifunctional version that always strives for Authentic Self Alignment and operates as is intended. Now, do not be discouraged if you still find times where you are faced with an emotion that triggers a Self disconnect; simply reconnect immediately, and you will find that this happens less and less frequently, until a disengagement of Authentic Self rarely occurs and is remedied instantaneously! In teaching you these things, we strive to show you who you truly are. We strive to show you that you are the Creator of your reality and that it is only your programming that makes you believe that you are separate from the true Divine Being you are. You are ready to exist as the True You. You are ready to exist as Self, operated by the one true programmer who has always been the programmer: YOU! You are ready to step into your power now!

So in saying this, let us now re-examine the creation process. A creation is initiated on the spiritual plane, advances through the mental plane and then proceeds to manifest on the physical plane. Let us examine in greater detail. You are always capable of manifesting the optimal creations for Self, ALWAYS. However, the data in your mind is also capable of distorting the abundant vibrational frequency of the optimal creative energy via your thoughts, as it passes through the Mental Plane. Thus, giving Self an authentic opportunity to experience Duality – unless one has overcome this illusion through reprogramming. Again, distortion is of no concern as it is a necessary part of the path to Conscious Realty Creation and causes no detriment to your desired creations. Distortion simply provides tangible evidence, showing you where your data needs to be upgraded so that you may then create what is truly desired moving forward. If you do not see the optimal version of your creation manifested before you, this indicates that a limiting belief has determined what you are allowed to have. Do NOT settle for anything less than the optimal resource you desire. You are not meant to – EVER. You are a Divine Creator, and you can have anything you desire. Do NOT allow your past programming, which was only essential to get you where you are now, to determine all of your creations. Embrace your power; embrace your knowing of your ability to manifest all that you desire. Allow nothing to hold you back. There is great power in simply knowing. There is great power in releasing all of your fears, all of your doubts and simply affirming that you have faith. The mind does not have all the answers. So no matter how hard you try to figure things out from a logical perspective, you will never find the answers. But Self knows; Self has the answers. As Authentic Self, you are capable of true knowing and of receiving all of the Joyous resources you will ever need for the rest of your physical existence. There are no limits; there is nothing that is out of reach. As Self, you will achieve your greatest dreams and reach your desired goals. As Self, you will see to it that the world is changed and your Heaven on Earth becomes a reality.

Before we end this lesson, we wish to bring a few things to your attention in preparation for what is to come. To begin, we wish to briefly address this concept that there is only ever the "now" or "present" and that you are only to live in the present. Although we do not negate the value of learning to truly live within What Is, many have used this concept of the "Present Moment" as a means to try to escape from the unwanted and the "bad," therefore, furthering the illusion of Duality. When the now is approached as a means to escape an unwanted past, it is this notion that creates an Attachment to the now AND to the past. The perception of a superior point in time creates a Dualistic concept suggesting that the present is somehow better than the past. But in reality, both concepts are neutral and one and the same. One is not superior to the other and one does not need to be denied for the other. Both are simply part of What Is. So from this perspective, we wish to impart upon you some new Truths about this concept of Time.

Firstly, time – as the majority of the physical world understands it – does not really exist. There is no present, there is no past and there is no future: AT ALL. These are simply created terms and concepts, which are a by-product of physical beings attempting to comprehend the truths of their existence from a physical perspective. In reality, this concept of passing time was a creation strictly for the physical worlds, to allow for the possibility of tangible physical analysis of growth and expansion. What is perceived as the passing of moments is merely expressions of What Is and has been intended. What Is appears measurable in the physical form, so that one may perceive the rise and fall of All That Is: life and death, moments coming and going, beginnings and endings. Such is a necessary perception to operate in a world of Duality and to immerse oneself in an authentic experience of growth. Tangible experiences that appear to follow a timeline are necessary to fully analyze one's development along the path of human existence. However, as a Conscious Creator, you must do away with these created labels and concepts related to time, as time has been misinterpreted by your senses and is simply an illusion. In reality, all that "was," "is" and "will be" is one and the same and simply What Is.

From a physical perspective, one perceives only physical existence and only tangible form and so the mind cannot deny the obviousness of What Is and the blatant appearance of passing moments of What Is. But in actuality, the appearance of passing "Time" was a creation for the physical worlds so that one could physically perceive development. You must understand time as such and not allow it to limit Self. Moving forward, you must acknowledge time as simply a created concept to chronologically order data for physical world growth and expansion. Time, from this enlightened perspective, is referred to as Chronological Time. Utilizing Chronological Time for cataloging purposes is not to be feared; it is simply a tool. However, to prevent limiting Self, the appropriate use of Chronological Time must be properly understood.

Analyzing Chronological Time to measure growth and expansion and determine what is desired moving forward is NOT an excuse to dwell on data or allow fears to project said data; hence, dragging you back into the illusion of time and ultimately causing distortion to your creations. No, this would be an inappropriate use of Chronological Time and will not serve you well as a Conscious Creator. But this thinking is precisely where many become trapped within this illusion of created time. They forget how essential past experiences are, and they create a "bad" concept out of a neutral resource simply designed for monitoring growth and expansion. They create this notion of a past dueling with the present and a future that hangs in the balance, waiting to be created as something that somehow exists outside of What Is in the current moment. Thus creating a concoction of fear as they struggle to avoid the past and live in a state of anxiety that the future will manifest as a creation beyond their control. They fail to see that time is not definite and does not hold any power over a Conscious Creator, as a Conscious Creator is a master of time and circumstances. You must see the truth of this concept of time. You must recognize that in reality, there is no division of time and there is only WHAT IS. For you see, what IS was built upon what was, and what will be is built upon what IS. And so all is connected and necessary. All is simply WHAT IS.

Allow us to expand upon this further. For the majority, they fail to see that Chronological Time is simply a means of analyzing moments of What Is to determine growth and expansion. And so many have continually trapped themselves into the illusion of what we call "Fractured Time." What was originally perceived as What Is - What Is passed, What Is occurring and What Is to come for growth and expansion - was grossly misinterpreted and fractured into three separate points in "Time." The past and future became separate concepts from the present – previous and future points in time that exist outside of the present, as supposedly separate points of attraction. From this separation stemmed great fear of the past, as one no longer understood its importance. From this misunderstanding sprang the desire to escape to the present in an attempt to hide from an unwanted past. And likewise, fear was created to accompany this concept of the future, as one forgot their ability to create and perceived upcoming moments of unforeseeable conditions.

But in reality, this is not the Truth of time. All perceived separate points in time – labeled as Past, Present or Future – are but one and the same; they are but moments of What Is appearing in a chronological order. The present is simply What Is and is an integration of ALL DATA from what is perceived as the past. Without every piece of the puzzle from the past, the present, as you currently perceive it, would not exist as it does. And so, one's past points of attraction and expressions of What Is, literally are the building blocks for the present and literally are the foundation of what Is all around you. The past and all of its data and experiences IS the present, for what was attracted in the past became the manifestations within the present. Likewise, the future will literally be What Is in the present moment. A future cannot exist without present intention, and as the present is built out of the past, the future is built out of the present. All perceived separation of time can collapse upon itself to the origin of What IS. For all that has ever been was an expression of What Is, and all that will appear to be MUST stem from What Is. Chronologically speaking, "What Is" is an amalgamation of what was from the perceived past and what has been intended for the perceived future. All exists as part of What Is.

Failing to see the truth of What Is causes the primary setback for Conscious Reality Creation. For when one fractures time, they perceive the future outside of the present and as something entirely separate. They create with the condition that what they desire will only exist in the "future" and fail to see that without accepting the desired as part of What Is in the present, it could never be in the future. They have allowed this illusion of Time to create conditions for their creations, and therefore, their desires will never be. For traditional Fractured Time does not accept the premise that the future is simply what is chosen in the present. Nor will it allow one to fully embrace the Truth that what is intended in the perceived present is now part of What Is and is now the coming future. From this limited perspective of Fractured Time, one sits and waits for their creation to be instead of accepting that it already IS. Instead of moving forward accepting what has been intended as what MUST BE manifested, they do not accept the creation as What Is in the present and so they will continually wait for a future that will never be.

In order to overcome the restrictions of Fractured Time, one must accept the Truth that the future IS the present and the past IS the present, and therefore, they exist one and the same – expressed as WHAT IS. One must come to see that what is perceived as a separation between past, present and future is simply the by-product of one's inability to comprehend the Truth of human existence and the connectivity and synchronicity of All That Is.

You must see beyond the illusion of the struggle of counterparts. You must see Chronological Time as a neutral resource and use it as such to simply order your experiences for analysis. Do not allow your Self to get trapped by illusory time, and as a result create unachievable conditions for your creations! Do not hide in the present as means to escape the past. The past is NOT bad. The past is the compilation of What Is and an essential ingredient to what you perceive to be the present. Do not fear the past believing that you must run from it, understand it and reprogram what your perceptions tell you about it. It is not to be escaped – it is to be embraced as part of What Is. In the same respect, you must never fear the future; for within acceptance of What Is lies the power to create all that you desire. See the Truth that all is simply What Is. Learn to truly live within What Is by accepting all aspects of your path – what was and what has been intended – as part of What Is for you now.

So in closing, know this: there is no past to get trapped within; there is only collected data that has and will continue to assist you on your path: an essential part of What Is. There is no future to fear, there is only the continual collection of Joyous data while incorporating all data that Is. There is no past or future that holds you; there is only data. There only IS. Do not strive to live within the present only; instead, see beyond the illusion of a separate "present" and strive to exist within What Is. Exist outside of the false notions of time. Exist within What Is and you will find your success as a Conscious Creator. There is nothing other than What Is, and What Is is ALL that is. See Fractured Time as part of the necessary illusion of the human path and as a key ingredient to the smoke and mirrors of the Dualistic World. We are finished with this most important subject, and we will recommence in the next lesson beginning the process of putting it all together.

LESSON 28
INTENTION

We will begin this lesson by going back to the beginning – back to our first lesson on understanding Energy. We take you back to the beginning so that we may address a very important part of the Reality Creation Process: Intention. If you recall from the first lesson, we indicated that the only difference between a table and a road is the Intention behind the use of the energy. In reality, both creations are made of precisely the same Source Energy and both creations are equal. The same applies to the physical form you see before you. This form is no better than the previously mentioned road or table, it is merely a representative of a different intention for the same energy. This is what we would like to discuss in this lesson, as we begin winding down and allowing for a full integration of the knowledge presented in this manual.

What is an intention exactly? It is a desire to see something through. Essentially, you willingly set a goal and you absolutely mean to see it completed. Well, this may represent the meaning behind the word, but intention to us means something far greater. Intention is the key to all creation. Intention is the desire that is set forth that determines the unique degree of vibrational frequency of that which you are creating. Allow us to explain further.

When an intention is set, it is this desire that then determines the exact vibrational frequency of the resource that is required. In other words, it is the intention that is the creation. To a master of manifestation, there is never anything other than an intention needed in the creation process. Visualizations are not necessary and neither are affirmations; they are simply tools to assist the physical aspect of Self. In reality, you need only intend for something to be and it is done. Remember, as we have indicated, you are not your body or your mind; you are YOU, the True You, a Divine Creator that is capable of providing all necessary resources for this physical experience. Where you find difficulty is in this disassociation with who you Truly Are.

Many of you start this Conscious Reality Creation Process thinking that you must chase after what you desire. You set your "Intentions," believing that what you must do is make YOUR SELF a vibrational match to the things that you desire. We are here to tell you today that in order to be the Conscious Creator of your entire reality, it is time to shed this belief. You do not need to make your Self a vibrational match to anything, as all resources are an extension of you. You do not need to focus on changing anything within you to match the frequency of a creation; you must simply set the intention for the resource that you desire and allow said creation – as a perfect match to YOUR vibration – to come to you. Simply put, you need not match the vibration of a creation; the creation must match your vibration. What you have created has been created for you, by YOU, via your Intention, and it is not something that exists outside of you.

It is coming from you and Source Energy. Believing that you must chase a creation, and implying that it is somehow separate from you, indicates that you do not trust in your ability to consciously create; nor do you understand the process. That which was created by you cannot match another, as it is created from your unique intention and holds a vibrational frequency that is a match to you alone. That which was created by another as a desired personal resources cannot be yours and vice versa.

So many of you focus your attention on forcefully trying to bring your creations into your experience by falsely believing that there is something inside of you that must change to match these specific creations. Remember, in reality, all creations are neutral, and everything is of the same Source Energy. There exists not a single thing in your world that is superior to another, and that includes your physical form. All form – in all aspects – is of the same Source Energy, which means that all creations exist on the same level. All creations are essentially the same and only exist as they do based on the intention for their existence. It is this intention that directs Source Energy into the things that you desire. Now, from this perspective, understand that there is nothing for you to make your Self a vibrational match to. All objects are created for you, by YOU, via intention. You are a Divine Creator, and it is within your power to direct Source Energy to suit the intention that you desire. Remember, everything that exists on the physical plane has been called forth by a Creator, as the Creator existed first – not the form.

What does this mean? Simply put, it is time to stop chasing your creations and understand that you are not required to work for them – they are required to work for you during this physical experience. All that exists on the physical plane exists to serve you in your experience of growth and expansion. There is nothing that exists that has not chosen to be, and all things that have come into physical form are serving a purpose. As a Divine Creator, you must see all creations for what they truly are – products of intention. So next time that you focus your attention on something that is wanted, let us say a new vehicle, know that you do not need to do anything other than determine through intention what is desired in a vehicle. You are to choose the color, the make and the features based on previously collected data. Then, you are simply to allow the vehicle to enter your physical reality, based on your intention for it. You are not to focus on a specific car and say, "Oh, I want this car so bad, so I need to change my thoughts and make myself a vibrational match to this specific car." You are not to think that the car is above you and your current experiences, for this is very detrimental to your power. You are to analyze data relevant to the desired creation, and you are to set an intention for your creation based on the optimal version for you. You are not required to choose from the limited options that you currently see before you in the physical, as these merely represent options to choose from. If what you see does not truly match your desires, trust in your creative abilities and customize a creation for YOU – knowing that it must be. Manifest the optimal creation for you and Source Energy will see to it that it manifests as YOUR creation. IT IS LAW.

Once you have customized your creation based on your unique data and determined the optimal match to your true desires, you are to set an intention of receiving. You are to say, "Okay, creation, I desire you in my experience so that I may relish in the Joy that you bring." That is all. You are not to try to figure out how you will get this car, and you are NOT to focus your attention on working so hard to adjust your vibrational frequency to be a match to what you desire. What you desire must match the vibrational frequency that you have set forth based on your intention! What you desire will be called forth and brought to you via your intention – such is the Universal Truth.

To further your understandings of intention, let us compare your desire for the experience of "material" items vs. other physical beings. The physical material items or objects such as cars, houses, clothing, money, etc. are simply resources – much the same as the beings you incarnate with. All that exists with you has chosen to come forth to assist you on your journey, and you have likewise chosen to come forth to assist them, representing a united intention to assist in growth and expansion on an individual level, for the ultimate expansion of the ALL! Material items differ from incarnated beings only because of intention! These objects have come forth to serve the intention of providing physical world comforts to assist you on your journey. These objects stem from the infinite life on your planet – springing forth from the Source – and are no less important than any incarnated being. They are simply a different expression of Source Energy brought forward via intention. While great growth and expansion is achieved through the obtaining and experiencing of objects – including one's rediscovery of the importance of ALL creations – man's greatest growth occurs through other incarnated beings. Man's greatest discovery comes from remembering the sacred connection between all life and ALL that exists. This reconnection begins with rediscovering the true origin of man and all animals that walk upon the planet. As one begins to understand their connection to other incarnated beings, they begin to see the same Source Energy within all. From connections with other physical beings – mammals, insects, birds, etc. included – all life forms are able to learn from one another and experience true love, compassion and Joy.

Through all resources that exist on the planet, one is able to rediscover the beauty that resides within all form. However, when analyzing available resources for growth, one can see that there is a blatant difference of intention between objects and physical beings. Objects are here to assist physical beings, without the obvious ability to be able to protest their use. Whereas other physical beings are also here to serve in individual growth and expansion, but as creators have the ability to choose. As creators, all beings have been fashioned with the intention to be able to direct their reality and all objects within their reality. They have also been given the ability to attract one another for growth and expansion. BUT in the case of all beings, there must be a co-creation that occurs to ensure that the experience is wanted by both parties. Again, in the case of objects – these creations have come forth as Source Energy choosing to play the role that you cast them in. They have chosen to play the props so that you may grow and expand and learn to recognize and appreciate ALL form as Source Energy. These creations are no different than us and are simply a different expression of the same Source Energy.

You possess the ability to direct Source Energy to manifest your will as the physical reality around you, and you also hold the ability to attract others looking for similar growth and expansion. As you work toward creating your Heaven on Earth, it is important to remember that you are given dominion over the reality around you; however, you must utilize this power with a great sense of understanding and compassion. You must appreciate all form for what it is, and you must always view it as sacred and of great importance. You must nurture your companionship with all other beings, as you will achieve your greatest growth this way, but you must always be respectful and understanding of the unique individual path of all other incarnated beings. You can draw another physical being to you, but you cannot direct their path nor determine what life they are to have. You are not to choose the destiny of another, and you are not to concern your Self with what another attracts.

As a Conscious Creator, you are to set your intentions for the resources you desire, and you are to allow said resources to come to you – whether they be objects or other physical beings. As you allow beings and objects to move into your life, you will find that others will fall away. Some will stay for a lifetime and others only a brief period, but all will be serving their function of assisting with your growth and expansion, and all will be receiving precisely the same assistance from you! So remember, it is most certainly true that you are a Conscious Creator, but you must embark upon this path understanding what it means to hold such power. You must walk forward today with a great sense of pride and understanding for the process, setting the optimal example for all.

Now, let us for a moment specifically discuss the creation of objects. Many look at object Reality Creation backward, thinking that it need be difficult to create the physical reality you desire. It is believed that you must focus all of your creative energy on something specific and make your Self a perfect vibrational match to each and everything you desire, one creation at a time. But in reality, this is never the case. In reality, you need only set intentions for all that you desire and then allow it to be so. There is no tedious work required to draw to you what you desire and so initiating multiple creations at one time is easy and very possible. You need only choose what is desired and allow your creations to manifest as a perfect vibrational match to what you have intended. You are not to worry about making your Self a match to anything. You are the Creative Being, not the objects that you are trying to attain. These objects are not masters that determine that you are now a match to them and so they will now happen into your experience. No, friends, your creations flow into your experience by your calling of them. All creations find their way into your experience, after being called forward by your intention. Your intention on the spiritual plane brings forth the thought that summons on the mental plane and ultimately manifests on the physical plane.

So please, brothers and sisters, do not allow your creations to master you. It is time to be a master of your creations and to embrace all the resources that exist on the physical plane to assist you! There is not a creation on the planet that has not been created for your use so that you may learn and grow and ultimately achieve your desired Ascension. All that exists on the physical plane exists as a resource available for you to experience.

Now that this is understood, let us compare this to the understandings achieved in the previous lesson. On the one hand, we have told you that you are the True You and that all creation stems from you! We have explained that all creations originate from the spiritual plane. We have explained that optimal creative Source Energy flows from the True You, and if it is not distorted by any limiting beliefs, it manifests as the optimal creation on the physical plane. Now, on the other hand, we have just told you that all exists as it was intended to be and that intentions are the key to creation. So in understanding this, where exactly does this intention come from? Is it the mind that sets the intention or is it YOU that sets the intention? Well it is YOU, of course! All intentions that come forth as a thought in the mind are the intentions that have been set forth by you, Higher Self! All "thought" intentions are simply a "heads up" to a desired creation that is on its way to you.

Allow us to expand upon this further. Suppose that you are going about your day, and you come across the data of a creation that triggers wonderful feelings of Joy on your Emotional Indicator. You determine that this is a creation that you would certainly love to experience. Within this desire and this Joyful response, an intention has been detected. An intention has been set forth by the True You, and it is has sprung forth as desire and as a thought to prepare the mind for the receiving of a new experience. At this moment, there are two possibilities: the mind is capable of allowing the optimal version of the creation, or as a result of limiting beliefs, the mind can distort the optimal frequency of the creative energy into something that is less desirable. If the mind is programmed to understand what all desire stems from, the mind will then proceed to create a visualization of the optimal desired resource, based on the previously collected data. During this visualization process, the mind focuses on the object, but it is not the object that sets the vibrational tone, it is the emotion associated with the experiencing of the object that creates the necessary vibrational frequency. For you see, through emotion, you find your creative focal point, and you set your sights only on what it is you desire. You focus so intently when enthralled by emotion. And whether this emotion feels pleasant or not, it is a powerful focused means of directing Source Energy, which will create whatever it is you are truly intending that much quicker. The vibrational output resulting from involved emotion is vastly more powerful than any lackluster thought, as emotion indicates belief, and belief indicates a clear intention of wanting and knowing what will be. Belief is at the heart of all physical creation, which is precisely why it is the emotion that is essential.

Through this visualization process, the mind is provided with optimal data indicating why a creation is desired. The mind is capable of playing out a vast array of experiences where one can "try on" a resource that is desired. But in reality, it is not the visualization of the resource itself that creates it at all – it is the intention to allow Self to receive the optimal resource. It is the intention to allow Self to receive whatever it is that is needed. This is precisely why many find that even after intending a specific creation, it does not come precisely as they imagined, but that in fact it has manifested as a version that serves them far more optimally then they previously imagined. The intention is the key, not focusing on the specific resource. The virtual resource is a guideline of sorts, but more accurately, simply conveys to Source Energy that you are now allowing your Self to receive all abundance and all resources that are meant for you. You can choose to focus on specific objects through visualizations, or you can simply choose to focus on receiving the optimal resources to assist you on your path via intention alone. It really matters not, the fact is the underlying intention will be to allow the optimal resources to assist you on your path. Your visualization tools are meant to assist you in conjuring in your mind's eye what the "optimal" version of your creation represents to you. This representation is merely a guideline, based on previously collected data, which sets the intention that you are allowing the optimal creation for you. It is the vibration produced via the visualization that attracts the optimal resource. It is the vibration, or more specifically the lack of resistance and distortion of Source Energy, that allows the optimal resource to flow! So dream BIG – choose the optimal resources in all of your experiences! Remember, intention is all that matters, and your visualizations are merely a tool to assist the mind in calling forth the optimal resources for Self. Visualizations merely give the mind a focal point to assist Self in the Conscious Reality Creation process. Set the Intention of abundance and acceptance of your power, and that is what will manifest around you! That is all that needs to be done, and in time, you will learn to create flawlessly and efficiently. You will receive the data through your senses, determine desire, and then you will proceed to allow the creation to manifest on the physical plane. You will not chase the creation and you will not seek it out; you will simply receive knowing and allow the creation to manifest, based on the intention set forth.

In the previous lessons, amidst the process of reminding Self how to consciously create, we presented you with visualization and affirmation tools. Although they are not necessary to the creation process, they provide opportunities to reconnect with the intentions set forth by YOU and allow you to produce the optimal vibration for the resources you desire. Again, these tools are not required to brainwash you, or force you to think a certain way; these tools are simply to allow you to realign with your true intention. Through these tools, you learn that you are not meant to settle for anything. You are not to look at the possibilities that exist around you and through your limited senses, say, "Okay, I guess I must choose between the only options I see." No, you must embrace your power as a Divine Creator; you must choose the creation that optimally serves you and then allow that creation to manifest before you. You are the Master. You are an aspect of the Source. You do not play by the rules of the physical world; you supersede them. And so when you create, dear friend, remember you are to aim for allowing the optimal intention. Because it is this intention – this true desire – which is creating. It is this intention that is directing Source Energy, and if you can create a mediocre resource or an optimal resource all the same, why would you not choose what serves you optimally at all times? Do not restrict your Self, and do not limit your power by believing that creation need be difficult. It is an easy process for you. Creations bend to your will and intention for them; not the other way around. There is no hard work to be done in the creation process; you need only determine the desired vibrational frequency and your creations will come to you!

While you move forward in your expansion, be understanding of this process, and know that it has not always been the intention of Self to know these things. It has not always been necessary to be a Conscious Creator, for you were not always ready for this step. You had to experience what you did, and you had to set intentions to deprive your Self of that which would optimally serve you so that Self would get to this exact point in time. You were not meant to always Consciously Create because that was not the intention for your growth. You were meant to learn, grow and expand and take every single necessary step until you reached this point of remembering. So, today, choose to step into the role of the Conscious Creator because the time has come for your intentions to shift. The time has come where you are ready to be who you have always truly been, and the time has come for you to set your example for the world.

Embrace this knowing. Move forward in your creative endeavors remembering all that we have taught you. Remember who it is that is creating. Remember that you are a mighty supreme being, a child of The All and ultimate Source, and you have this all figured out. Choose the reality that you desire and move forward knowing that it will be. Recognize the illusion of time, and see that once you choose for something to be, it is done via your intention. For what is chosen in the present must be in the future, as the future is simply choice within the present. Live each moment forward believing wholeheartedly that what you desire will come and that you will always have the resources you need. Know that the moment it is intended is the moment it is done; for what is written in the present, is the future that will come. You must believe it and choose it in the present for it to be. Choose it now and live every moment, speak every word in correlation with the intention you have set. Believe it wholeheartedly because you have chosen for it to be and so it must be.

Always remember, through choice we are granted our greatest desires, and by the hand of The All our will is done on Earth, as it is in the Heavens. Through Intention, it is written, and through The All, it is given.

That is all for today. We will recommence in the next lesson teaching you how to master your Senses. In doing so, you will see the world for what it truly is and allow your Self to live outside the box.

LESSON 29
EXPANDING YOUR SENSES

As we wind down these lessons and finalize the last of your new understandings, we do so with a great sense of pride. We take great Joy in the process of teaching you, and we are eager to see you utilize what we have awakened within you to change the world. There is no doubt that you will be successful, as it is your utmost intention to succeed. There is no failure, as failure is not an option for Self – only success! We will continue on with our second last lesson, and we will do so with absolute pride in our student, knowing the wonderful changes brewing within you.

Today, we are going to delve deeper into this concept of physical senses. We are going to focus primarily on what the senses are for and how to use them correctly. As we indicated at the very beginning of these lessons, your senses have deceived you. Now please understand in us saying this, we do not imply that this deception was valueless. For we know that everything that happened to you and every piece of data accumulated was collected for a purpose. There was nothing that was unplanned and not crucial to your path. So in saying that your senses have deceived you, we do not imply any sort of malicious intent

– to the contrary, in fact. Your senses have deceived you, as they were meant to. You were meant to collect every bit of the essential data that exists within your mind and the Collective Mind. You were meant to see it through so that you could find your Self at this precise point in time, on the precipice of great change. You have seen the Truth of who you are. You understand your creative abilities, and you have acquired great knowledge. So where do you go from here? Well, today, we want to remind you how to use your senses correctly so that you may move forward operating Self as is intended for the optimal physical experience. We want to remind you how to use all of the assets and resources available to you, to create the most glorious and splendid version of your reality. We want to remind you how to use your senses to create your Heaven on Earth!

Let us recap. What are the senses exactly? Well, the senses – touch, taste, smell, sight and hearing – are your five basic senses. You should be very familiar with the basic five. These are the senses that operate as your Data Collection Tools. These are built-in instruments designed to allow you to fully experience your reality and collect data with various results. As we indicated previously, these are your basic senses. You have also been equipped with a sense less commonly acknowledged and known as your sense of Feeling. Simply put, your sense of Feeling allows you to feel your environment. Now let us explain; this has nothing to do with your sense of touch. No, to feel is to acknowledge that which cannot be experienced by the other senses. To feel is to pick up on the energetic impressions of all that exists in your reality. You see, as you are well aware by now, everything in your reality offers a vibrational pulse as everything in your reality is of the same Source Energy.

And so there is nothing that does not offer this vibrational connection.

You have the most marvelous ability to sense these energetic frequencies, which are evident in all that exists on the physical plane. Using your sense of feeling correctly, you can allow your Self to sense the emotions, the physical state and even the vitality of all that exists around you. You can pick up on the anger or Joy of another physical being, or you can even detect a state of disease within in a tree. Your ability to feel energetic impulses allows you to view the world in a completely different light. You not only view the world with your five basic senses, but you also see the world for what it truly is – vibration! Through acknowledging and interpreting this vibration, you are able to fully understand your reality. You are capable of gaining an inside peak into all that exists around you, on more than just a superficial level. All beings that exist at higher levels of consciousness have mastered this ability to feel and can very easily detect the energetic impressions produced by all that exists on your planet. We are able to determine through these impressions precisely what healing is needed – or more accurately, what resistance is being presented. In realizing these things, we are then able to customize our assistance to provide optimal healing. Now, imagine what you would be capable of doing if you were able to view the world in such a manner! You would instantly know the concerns of another, you would instantly recognize the pleas of nature, and you would find a connection with ALL THAT IS, so undeniable and earth changing that you would never be the same. So how do you achieve this connection; how do you sense this energetic flow? Well, through intention, of course. That is where you must begin. By intending that it be so!

Before we get into the basics of how to use your sense of feeling to assist others, let us discuss on a personal level how using all six of your senses can be beneficial in your own life! When you create, you do so using the data collected by the senses. All desire stems from what you have seen, heard, etc. and this data is then used to initiate the desires of Self. Data is an essential part of the creation process, for if you did not learn what you desired to have there would be nothing to desire. And so from this perspective, one can see how the senses are essential to your creation process. Now, in order to use the senses optimally, you must embrace what data the senses are meant to be collecting. Any and all data serves you well, but when you are ready to become a Conscious Creator, you can choose which data you give your attention to. You can make the conscious choice to simply search for data of a Joyous nature. This is not to say that you need to run away from data that is not Joyous – to the contrary. You must never be afraid of data, for it is merely a neutral option to choose from. But you must see these creations of "undesired" data as simply a starting point to then determine what data is desired. You must take what is perceived as undesired and from it search for the Joyous emotion, hence, determining what varying degree of the creation is suitable for your desired state of Joy. Remember, you do not determine your Joy based on the creation, rather, the creation is determined based on your Joy. You are to always search for the optimal Joyous feeling and, in doing so, then determine which creation/resource and ultimately data, best serves you in achieving this Joyous state. These creations – or data – will constantly change, but your search for Joy never will.

Make finding Joy your ultimate goal, and you will achieve the ability to allow creations to flow freely and easily, in and out of your experience as they are needed.

You must understand that all of these creations are but data for the mind; they are but resources to allow you to achieve the desired state of Joy. And once they have been obtained, you will use this data to then determine what is now desired to achieve the desired state of Joy. It will be an ongoing, never ending experience of seeking Joy and utilizing resources to achieve it! You must come to an understanding that all experiences and all desired creations are data that assists you in determining what you would like to experience – nothing more or nothing less. All that you desire to have is obtainable by Self and must begin in the data collection stage.

When you collect the necessary data and receive an energetic impression from your sense of Feeling, indicating that this will provide the optimal vibrational frequency and be in alignment with Joy, you have now determined where your attention must lie. But remember, it is not the resource or creation that has an optimal vibration. In fact, this vibration is really no different than any other varying degree of the creation. What you are feeling in terms of the optimal Joyous vibration is the indication from Higher Self signaling that this creation is a resource desired to optimally assist Self and to bring about the experience of Joy. Again, it is not the creation itself that brings the Joy, it is the utilization of the creation. This creation alone, without utilizing it, would not serve you. But the utilization of the creation will allow you to experience something required for your path that is new and exciting; this is what ultimately brings you Joy.

You must remember that there are no creations that are superior in this process; you must remember the neutrality of All That Is. Simply search for the data that triggers the Joyous feeling, indicating that this is a desired experience for growth and expansion and ultimately the overall collection of data. In doing so, you will further propel your Self on your path of desires. This is a most Joyous understanding to come to – that all of your senses exist to simply allow you to browse through an extensive catalog, choosing that which brings you the most Joy. Essentially, finding that which makes your heart sing and simply saying, "Yes, I want this, and yes, I want that!" It may sound far too good to be true, but that is precisely the way it works. You are to use your senses to determine what is desired. You are then to take the desired data, and through focusing on the vibration of it for even a brief period of time, allow your desire to become part of your reality as a clear and undisputed vibrational frequency. This clear intention will then attract the manifestation of a tangible creation on the physical plane. Remember, as we indicated before, your creations come to you; they are a match to you. As a Conscious Creator, you do not need to do any work to make your Self a match to anything. You choose what is desired, you create the vibrational frequency, and you simply allow it to flow into your experience. That is all!

In understanding this, begin to utilize your senses correctly; begin to collect your data and place your order. Do not doubt your ability to simply acknowledge what is desired and allow it to be. Remember, you ARE Source Energy! The same energy that orchestrates physical form, flows continuously through the True You and to your physical form to create whatever reality you desire. This same energy could create your greatest nightmare or your greatest desire; the choice is yours. If you want your dream, your Heaven on Earth, simply choose for it to be so. Simply choose to embrace your creative abilities, and choose to accept how it is that you create. You are a Divine Being, capable of creating anything you desire, and you are a Master of all that exists around you. You choose what resources you need, and you choose what data serves you. Do not allow data that does not assist you as a Conscious Creator to prevent you from having what you desire, for to do so is simply preposterous. It is but data that you simply no longer desire to experience. So make your choice. Choose the data that serves you and that you wish to experience as part of what IS in your reality. Do not be afraid; you CAN do this! We will end our discussion on this subject and recommence in the following lesson, further expanding on your ability to feel and how to connect with All That Is.

~Shine your light Advocate of Truth. Shine it for all to see and set your own example of Heaven on Earth, so that you may encourage others to do the same. Encourage individual growth and expansion - encourage uniqueness. Embrace the differences on your planet. Do your part in creating Heaven on Earth by encouraging others to create their own essential and unique versions.~

LESSON 30
MOVING FORWARD

We are most pleased to have reached this final lesson. Although it may seem like the end of our discussions, this is truly only the beginning. As you continue to expand and grow and allow in more and more data, we will remain beside you assisting you on your path until the day you return to your true form. We will never leave your side – ever! So please know moving forward, that you go on with mighty companions beside you – mighty companions that will love and care for you always. Remember, dearest brothers and sisters: when you seek a helping hand, you need only ask for our assistance.

We will carry on with the understandings discussed in the previous lesson. Allow us to briefly recap what has been discussed thus far. You understand that your senses are wonderful tools for extensive data collection. You embrace that this data is essentially what fuels the version of Self you are operating as and recognize that it is the mind that regulates the use of said data. You understand that as a Conscious Creator you have access to all information ever collected by Self, and you now choose to master the mind; you now choose to meticulously select which data you would like to utilize.

You have assumed the role of Authentic Self, and you are the Master of your mind and all circumstances that enter into your reality. Today, we would like to expand on these understandings.

From what we have told you thus far, you should have come to the realization that your senses can not be used optimally without an understanding of what they are truly meant to do. The senses were created so that you could collect data and recognize that which brings you Joy. Now, what we would like to expand on is what this Joy is really all about. Joy is not something that is interchangeable between one person and another. This is not to say that one would not find Joy in the experiences of another, but the level of Joy and the experience altogether would vary from person to person, dependent on the individual perspectives. Why is this? Why is your Joy the only Joy that is relevant to you? Why is the same concept of Joy experienced so differently from person to person? Why is it that Joy matters so much in the physical? Well, the answer is simple: because this detection of Joy is your built-in Emotional Indicator, informing you that what you are experiencing is desired for your path and ultimately for growth and expansion. So what does this mean? This means you can do away with the notion that Joy is anything other than a signal for Self, indicating that an experience is desired. You can do away with the fears that tell you what you desire is wrong, and you can do away with any sense of disappointment from not finding Joy where another finds Joy. The fact is, you are not meant to follow anyone else's path, so why would you find Joy in precisely what another finds Joy in? It simply could not be.

Your path is unique to your own individuality, and this is, as it must be, for the expansion of All That Is. Every individual existence must be different to provide their much needed, wonderful perspective to the collective. So please remember, dear brothers and sisters, your Joy does not indicate anything other than a desire from the True You to experience something for growth and expansion. It is time to stop looking to others for what brings them Joy in hopes that it will trigger something within you. Know this: your path is unique to you, and as a Conscious Creator you must find – you must seek out – the events, objects and people that will trigger your Emotional Indicator and inform you of the next Joyous step to take! Joy is not some mystical goal to try and reach. Joy is not something that is found only in "spiritual practices," in yoga or mediation or long walks on the beach. Joy is dependent on your individual path and your individual required resources for your path. So please, do not chase another's dreams; do not allow your limiting belief of Perfectionism to keep you from experiencing your own Joy and ultimately the required resources to assist you on your path. You see friends that is all Joy is. It is a triggering of your Emotional Indicator, informing you that you have encountered a resource, a teacher or a desired experience to assist you on your path of achieving growth and expansion. It is really that simple.

This concept of Joy has been misunderstood for centuries, and as a result, so many of you have created Attachments to the concept. You seek what others have told you will bring Joy, and you have forgotten what Joy is actually indicating: a resonance with your individual path. So moving forward, allow your Self to embrace this knowing. Allow your Self to seek out the Joy that is desired for you! Allow us to work together on this; allow us to assist you in keeping your focus on your individual path so that you may allow your Self the resources required to assist the world! When we talk so frequently about your own path and following your own Joy, please understand that we do not say this so that you focus only on your Self and not the world. What you fail to see is that you working on your Self IS working on the world. Your example of Joy and peace is what will change the world. Your mental control and peaceful thoughts will cause a shift so great in the collective that the world will finally know the peace that it so desperately seeks. Through your example, and attainment of your piece of Heaven on Earth, you will show others the Truth of who they truly are. You will shine a light so bright that not one will be able to deny the true reality of human existence. Do not be afraid to find your Joy and follow your own path, because it is only in doing so that you will truly change the world.

In concluding these lessons, we believe it is most essential that you fully grasp the potential of your senses and understand how to use them optimally. It is most important that you recognize the great power you hold and learn to interpret the energy that you receive correctly and without harm to your Self. The first thing you must come to understand about energy is that it is everywhere – IT IS everything, and so you are constantly going to be receiving signals indicating what is desired on your path. Along with this receptivity comes the ability to connect with the energy of others. This natural born gift can be used to assist, but if not understood correctly, it can also be used as a form of torment for Self. For you see, many come to a point where they begin to feel the energies of those around them so fiercely that they are no longer able to separate themselves from that which they are perceiving.

Allow us to explain further. As an example: when one is around another who is angered, the anger and the energetic frequency omitted as a result of said anger is protruding from the individual in their auric field. It is pouring from them and affecting their surroundings. For those like you that are empathic and are easily, but often unknowingly, utilizing their built-in energy receptors, they are going to detect this energy and feel it much easier than others. However, instead of Feeling it and understanding that it belongs to another, the empathic individual goes into defense mode and essentially panics and absorbs the energy as their own! It is not necessary to do so, but for one that does not understand energy and the nature of the empathic body, it is very easy to leave one's Self defenseless. And so in this particular case, the individual has a negative reaction to the perceived energy – informing Self via the Emotional Indicator that this is not a desired state of being. Instead of Self recognizing the energy as simply received impressions, Self instantly takes on the energy and chooses to allow it to take over their own energetic field.

Now, what must first and foremost be understood about this scenario is that it is a choice – a choice that is always made by Self! There is no one outside of you forcing anything upon you, as this concept is against law. There is simply energy that can or cannot affect you based on your attraction of it. And so, you must remember that it is your choice to allow this transference or not. All that is truly required in this moment of perceived undesired energy is to simply acknowledge it for what it is and set the very powerful objective to remain in a vibrational state of abundance and natural well-being. The conscious choice to understand what is occurring – and supersede it – is ALL that is needed. So many will create a struggle in their own minds to fight the anger within themselves, but to that we say you are simply playing into Duality. Do not fight any part of you and scream at it as though it is bad. It is all a part of you – a beautiful necessary part – and you are in control of every single aspect of YOU. If anger is felt, you can so very easily make the choice to transmute it into a natural abundant state of well-being. It is all a matter of choice!

Many of you understand this term "Empath" and yet you do not embrace the grand meaning of this concept. Your empathic ability is simply your natural talent to connect to the energy of all living things on your planet. This does not simply mean human beings, this includes the animals, the trees, the waters and the Earth. Every living thing on your planet has a unique vibrational frequency, and you can, so very easily, use your senses to tap into these frequencies. In fact, many of you do this already by sensing the anger of another before they have even spoken a word or finding your Self feeling uncomfortable around another even though you know nothing about them. These are your senses picking up on their vibration. Remember, these people are not "bad" or "evil," they simply offer a different vibration from yours, as do all living things on the planet. So, how does this relate to our understandings presented previously? Well, simply put, using your empathic abilities allows you to connect to others and determine: firstly, if they are a resource or teacher desired for your path and secondly, if there is information to assist them on their path. Know that the latter is a skill that takes time, but can most certainly be done. When the fear of allowing another's state of well-being to affect you subsides, you are capable of focusing solely on the energy of another and fully understanding their reality without taking it on as your own. When this state is achieved, you will be able to appreciate the current attractions, emotional state and well-being of another simply by connecting with their energy. It may sound complicated, but it is truly not – it is a practice that flows naturally for ALL once fear and distraction are removed and the knowing is allowed to flow.

So know this, simply because you encounter another living being that does not resonate with your path, based on your Emotional Indicator signaling that no further experiences are desired, this does not mean that there isn't something that can be done to assist this being. Do not shut your Self away from this person; instead, be an example. Through your energy, they will resonate Joyously with your being. They will attract to you and the vibration that you offer. Through your example, you will provide a resonance within them. Your energetic expression will trigger their Emotional Indicator, telling them that something within you is desired. If you do not resonate with the vibration of another being, you do not need to run away or even seek further experiences with this person. You need only embrace the current experience and know that your encounter with them may not have been for your benefit, in the way you might perceive. This encounter has served the purpose of providing an example for them and an opportunity for you to shine a much needed light. Although you may not resonate with their energy, it does not mean that you cannot still be of service. Through this interaction, while you provide a much needed example to them, you will ultimately find your Joy.

So remember, beautiful friend, in all that you do, you have the opportunity to set an example. While you seek out your Joy so that you may determine what resource or teacher is required, you are presented with the opportunity to help others. You are not asked to merely focus on your path and ignore all others; you are to find the Joy in ALL experiences that you encounter and, in doing so, set a mighty example for ALL. If you do not feel it, seek it out because each experience is ripe with opportunities of Joy attempting to provide the resources to assist you and further you on your path. Turn no one away as a suitable candidate to be an example for, but remember to be accepting of their own Joys and their own path. Remember, your way is not the right way; your way is simply the right way for you, and the best way to assist others, is to simply be you!

Your greatest gift to others is through your example of Joy and acceptance! When you learn to hone your energetic receptors, you will come to an understanding that another is not responsible for your emotional state and well-being – YOU ARE. You will realize that you are most efficient in assisting the world when you are NOT shutting anyone out. You will see that by understanding your capability to control your own emotional state, you can provide an optimal example to ALL. You are not to hide or run away, you are to be seen and to be visible! You are to show the world that, through practice and dedication, one can learn to achieve a state of peace where others do not affect their well-being. Where one can truly understand another and, in doing so, affect negativity in a positive and productive way. When this is understood, the world will see that you can change the lives of others without forcing individual views and beliefs upon them. You can show them a different way by simply being who you are and standing in your own power! You can show others that acceptance, understanding and peace is all that is required to change the world!

Before we end this lesson, we wish to impart upon you one last and most important understanding. Along your journey of seeking out Joyous data, you will encounter moments of contrast, moments where you might find it a struggle to remain in Authentic Self Alignment. We encourage you to not be alarmed and to simply remember your teachings. This is an indication that you have encountered limiting programming, and there is a limiting belief that must be Recognized, Analyzed and Re-Strategized. What we would like to impress upon you now is how to recognize what has triggered your Emotional Indicator and if this triggering is from contrast or resonance. Although any triggering of your Emotional Indicator verifies how data relates to your higher purpose, there is a vast difference between a triggering that is merely indicating your resonance with a creation to determine if said creation is a desired resource vs. a triggering where contrast is felt, indicating that reprogramming is required. You must learn to recognize the difference between the two. The difference is felt within your knowing, and you will find that when contrast occurs it is impossible to keep your thoughts off of that which produced the conflict. Contrast simply signifies an incompatibility between programming: i.e. incompatibility between outdated Self programming and Self 2.0 programming. Simply put, the data that is causing the contrast is triggering your Emotional Indicator, telling you that this data must be upgraded. Therefore, contrast is simply an "error sign" in your new programming. This sign must be acknowledged as such and Self must allow the programmer, the True You, to reprogram the data to run a more efficient Self 2.0.

You must recognize that the contrast and reprograming segments of your path are not to be feared. This is an indication that you have reached a point on your journey where you have achieved wonderful understandings, which are now allowing you to identify the "error signs" in your Self programming. This is simply an indication that you have received the necessary programing, and you are now prepared to move beyond this limiting data that is presenting contrast. This is not a failure on your part or an indication that you have digressed or done anything wrong. This is absolutely not the case. In fact, this is an indication that you are doing everything right. Your ability to distinguish the reason for the triggering of your Emotional Indicator and your ability to recognize that clarity, or new data, is required to eliminate the contrast – IS a testament to your vast knowledge and advancement in consciousness!

When you fully allow your Self to embrace and practice these knowings, you will undoubtedly find complete Joy in the data collection process. You will understand that perceived difficulties do not have to be a struggle at all. They can be accepted for what they are: periods of data collection for necessary growth and expansion. Regardless of the situation you find your Self in, clarity will always bring you peace.

Lastly, we wish to remind you that you should not expect your Self to be perfect; for the process of data collection takes a lifetime. The moment you cease to collect data on the physical plane, is the moment you depart the physical world. Moving forward, remember that data collection is nothing to fear as it is simply part of your continual growth and expansion. When you are faced with an experience that produces contrast and discomfort on your Emotional Indicator, do not fear. For this is simply an opportunity to collect essential data to your path of being an advocate for the light of Truth. This experience was attracted by Self, for the overall growth of Self, and it is through overcoming this limiting data that you set an example for all. So remember, when you trigger resistance, do not fight with more resistance or you will only create like thoughts and prevent the reprogramming process. Instead, be confident in your knowing and acknowledge that there is something to be learned and data to be received. Allow Self the patience and the necessary time to collect the required data to transmute that which no longer serves you. Embrace the knowing that there are no "bad" experiences, only essential experiences for growth and expansion. Please know, creating your Heaven on Earth does not mean ceasing to grow and collect new data, which is often achieved through briefly experienced contrast. It means finding peace and Joy within the process of data collection – or more simply put: the beautiful experience of being human.

We have so greatly enjoyed our time together. This has been a rewarding experience for us and we look forward to carrying on with you, in all of your endeavors. May the light within you shine brightly for all to see. May you change the world with every thought, word and action – and in doing so, bring peace upon the earth. We applaud you for all that you do and for being an advocate for the change that the world is now ready to receive. We will be watching and will be ready to assist you whenever you should call upon us. Be strong, have faith in your abilities and create your Heaven on Earth!

In love and light,
The Brotherhood of Light

GLOSSARY

ALL THAT IS – An expression used to convey the connectedness of ALL that exists. All That Is, is a representation of Source Energy and all things physical and nonphysical alike that stem from The Source.

ASCENSION – A stage in Self Expansion where one overcomes the illusions of the physical world, therefore allowing themselves to see beyond physical world limitations and live in pure connectedness to All That Is. Once a being of ascended consciousness completes their desired growth and expansion from their physical lives, they will graduate from "physical world school" and ascend to a new form of being.

ATTACHMENT – The means by which one becomes emotionally bonded to their creations. This dependency is always fear based and stems from dualistic thinking. An Attachment to a creation prevents one from focusing their intention elsewhere.

AUTHENTIC SELF – The true connection of Self, consisting of an aligned Body, Mind and Soul. Authentic Self connection occurs beyond duality and is the closest to existing as one's true nonphysical Self.

BODY – The physical form representation of Self. The body is the means by which Higher Self experiences physical existence and tangible reality. The body is a data collection apparatus, as well as a communication tool for Higher Self.

CHRONOLOGICAL TIME – The means by which one chronologically orders time for the purpose of cataloging events. Fractured time – Past, Present and Future – is an illusion currently practiced by the masses but does not exist beyond the physical world. The illusion of time exists merely for physical world reality as a means to track and analyze growth and expansion.

CLARITY – The necessary collection of data required to operate a desired upgraded version of Self. Clarity is required when Self has not yet obtained the necessary data to allow a new creation, eliminate liming beliefs, develop a new ability, etc.

COLLECTIVE MIND/CONSCIOUSNESS – The collective of all individual consciousness. The Collective Mind is comprised of all collected data and every thought, desire and intention set forth by any physical being who has been or currently exists. It is the means by which the planetary program runs, allowing all individuals to co-exist with each other while respecting individual points of attraction.

CONSCIOUS CREATOR – An obtainable version of Self that allows one to ascend beyond dualistic thinking and master time and circumstances. A Conscious Creator is fully capable of directing all experiences and resources to match their desire for a Joy-based existence.

CONTRAST – An indication that clarity – i.e. data – is needed to upgrade the current version of Self. Contrast triggers uncomfortable emotions via one's Emotional Indicator, signaling that the mind is not equipped with the necessary data. Contrast is an indication of a discrepancy between old programming and new programming. It is a clear indicator that reprogramming is needed to eliminate resistance and receive the necessary data required for growth and expansion.

DATA – Programming that is responsible for producing the individual aspect or "personality" of Self. Data is collected throughout one's entire physical existence to create desire and result in a growing and ever expanding version of Self.

DUALITY – The perception of opposites in opposition. Duality is the dominant illusion of the physical world and leads physical beings to perceive all creations as either "good" or "bad," thus creating Attachment. Duality is a created measure to ensure an authentic physical learning experience necessary to keep one blinded from who they truly are so that they may achieve authentic growth and expansion.

EGO SELF – The dual aspect of Self, created for an authentic experience of both the "light" and "dark." The Ego Self does not exist beyond ascension and is merely a creation for the physical world experience.

EMOTIONAL INDICATOR – A built-in indication system that guides the physical aspect of Self. When utilized optimally, it signals limiting beliefs and informs Self when reprogramming is needed. As a Conscious Creator, one is also capable of using this indicator system to determine what is desired on one's Joy-based path.

EMPATHIC – The ability – whether known consciously or not – to energetically connect with the physical world. Those that are empathic were born with this ability or have intentionally amplified their energy receptors, which are built into every human at a cellular level.

FEELING/FEEL – The sixth sense that allows physical beings to energetically connect with reality. All humans are born with built-in energy receptors that exist at a cellular level. As one expands in consciousness, they are able to heighten this sense of feeling to optimally connect with others, as well as determine the optimal resource to assist them on their path.

FREE WILL – A concept created to express Higher Self's choice to experience duality in the physical world. Free will exists for Higher Self and is expressed through the mind – the operating system of Self that allows for the experience of "good" and "bad" on the physical plane.

GOD – A word representing the infinite energy and consciousness that exists within all things and governs All That Is. The Source. See: SOURCE CREATOR/SOURCE ENERGY

HIGHER SELF/SOUL – The infinite aspect of Self that exists as a nonphysical being. Higher Self is the True You and the one experiencing physical existence through the mind and body of Self.

JOY – The optimal emotion one can feel that is in alignment with your most natural state of being. For a Conscious Creator, Joy is an indication of a desired resource for your path.

LIMITING BELIEF – Programming, or data, that has been collected that limits the power and potential of Self.

MIND – The operating system of Self that runs the current version of "YOU" and your physical reality. The mind houses all received data and directs Source Energy into the physical reality you perceive, based on your underlying beliefs and intentions.

NEUTRALITY/NON-DUALITY – A state beyond the illusion of opposites in opposition. Neutrality allows one to see the true origins of all physical creations and to understand that all stems from Source as a neutral option to choose from. When one ascends into a non-dualistic mindset, they understand that "good" and "bad" is merely a matter of individual perception and that ALL is choice for growth and expansion.

PAST LIVES – The "previous" physical aspects of Higher Self. As physical existence is an opportunity for growth and expansion, most beings have experienced numerous lives in a physical reality, playing various different roles.

PHYSICALITY – Existence as a physical being.

REALITY CREATION – The process by which one creates the physical world that is seen before them. Physical reality is produced either consciously or unconsciously via the dominant data in one's mind that directs Source Energy. As a a Conscious Creator, one has reprogrammed the data within their mind and is a master of their thoughts. As a result, they are consciously able to direct Source Energy to manifest their Joy-based desires.

RESOURCES – The means necessary for a physical existence. As a Conscious Creator, you are capable of choosing the optimal resources for your path, be it food, clothing, knowledge, finances, etc.

SELF – The union of Body, Mind and Soul. Self is the means by which one is able to experience growth and expansion in a physical reality.

SENSES – The means by which one collects data in the physical world. The senses allow humans to perceive physical reality from different perspectives and, as a result, obtain well-rounded growth and expansion.

SOURCE CREATOR/SOURCE ENERGY – The origin and building blocks of all that exists in the physical and nonphysical. The Source is the true consciousness that gives life to all extensions of consciousness. The Source is All That Is.

TRUE YOU – The infinite creator that exists beyond physical reality.

WHAT IS – An expression used to convey what exists as part of one's reality. What Is, is a culmination of all that has been intended, whether currently perceived in the physical or not.

ABOUT THE AUTHOR

Amanda is a wife, mother and channel who joyfully balances her time between personal and global passions.

Through Family of Light Teachings, Amanda brings forward a vast array of inspirational material and resources designed to assist fellow awakened beings on their journey. Utilizing the teachings of the Universal Truths Manual, Amanda has developed the Universal Truths Workshop™ and fulfills her own teaching passion as a Self Expansion Coach™. She is dedicated to supporting others through the Self Expansion experience so that they may step into their power and see to it that the universal dream of peace on Earth is realized!

Visit **www.familyoflightteachings.com** to view additional channelled material and learn about services and upcoming workshops!

FAMILY OF LIGHT TEACHINGS

Made in the USA
Middletown, DE
27 May 2015